Twist

MARTHA COLLISON

For Mum, Dad and Hannah

HarperCollins*Publishers*
1 London Bridge Street, London, SE1 9GF

www.harpercollins.co.uk

First published by HarperCollins*Publishers* 2016

A catalogue record of this book is available from the British Library.

ISBN: 978-0-00816826-1

Food styling: Annie Rigg
Prop styling: Liz Belton

Printed and bound in China

MIX
Paper from
responsible sources
FSC™ C007454

FSC™ is a non-profit international organisation established to promote the
responsible management of the world's forests. Products carrying the FSC
label are independently certified to assure consumers that they come from
forests that are managed to meet the social, economic and ecological needs
of present and future generations, and other controlled sources.

Find out more about HarperCollins and the environment at
www.harpercollins.co.uk/green

Twist

Creative Ideas to Reinvent Your Baking

MARTHA
COLLISON

HarperCollins*Publishers*

CONTENTS

INTRODUCTION

When I was eight years old, I was given my first recipe book as a Christmas present.

Inspired by the big, child-friendly pictures, I pulled out my step-stool and got my hands straight into my first ever bake: rock cakes. As I pulled the dense, slightly charred lumps from the oven, my family smiled doubtfully then politely gulped down the dry crumbs, hoping that baking would be just another childish phase.

However, as time went on, batch after batch of different rock cakes would come out of our old, unpredictable oven. I'd mix in whatever I could find, from chocolate buttons to pink sprinkles to dried fruit. Every recipe was an adventure and I fell in love with baking.

I approached recipes as something to inspire new creations rather than as a set of rules to be followed; they were beginnings rather than endings. I wanted to understand how a recipe worked, what to do when it went wrong, and what roles different ingredients have to play. Understanding the science behind baking, along with my curiosity, has given me the confidence and freedom to bake anything. Being part of series 5 of *The Great British Bake Off* required all of that confidence, and through the recipe development and competition stages I learnt a huge amount about designing and creating exciting bakes. Appearing on the show threw me headfirst into the world of food writing and experimental baking, and I have enjoyed it so much I hope I never have to leave!

And, although I've come a long way from basic rock cakes, teaching myself all manner of baking techniques over the last ten years, the essence of my baking is the same: I still approach recipes with the same curiosity. This book contains the results of that curiosity; it features many of my favourite recipes, along with unique twists and variations for you to try. The recipes have short twists; others are full-length ones. And there are also some twists on classic bakes.

I've also included evolution diagrams of some key recipes, which guide you through how I choose and match complementary flavours in my baking and how it is possible to adapt and vary a basic recipe to make something completely different. Once you've mastered the basics and understand how the flavours work, whether for a sponge, pastry or meringue, you can create your very own twists – the possibilities of what you can create are endless.

Whatever your ability and whether you've never baked or been baking for years, I want to show you how easy it is to produce modern, delicious bakes.

Martha

x

EQUIPMENT

CAKE TINS

For round cakes, the tins I use most frequently are 18cm and 20cm. Avoid the shallow sandwich tins; you want loose-bottomed, deep tins for cakes that are easy to remove. Ideally, you want three tins in each size, but one tin will be enough if you bake the cakes in batches. I buy pre-cut circles of baking parchment because I really hate lining tins – these make it a lot quicker and easier!

Other useful tins to have are a 20 x 30cm traybake or brownie tin, a 1-litre metal loaf tin and a circular bundt tin. You will also need a 12-hole muffin tin to make cupcakes. I tend not to use silicone bakeware because it is harder to work with and more difficult to remove cakes from. It can also change baking times, as silicone doesn't conduct heat in the same way as metal.

To make tarts I use a round 23cm tin with a removable base. You could invest in mini tartlet tins to make smaller tarts, if you like.

BAKING TRAYS

I normally line mine with a reusable non-stick baking sheet to reduce waste. If you don't have one, baking parchment will work just as well.

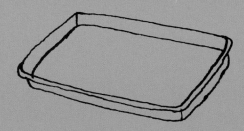

MIXING BOWLS

Glass, ceramic and metal bowls are superior to plastic, as plastic bowls can sometimes retain a film of fat, even after washing. They are heatproof and dishwasher-safe, making them a great choice for baking. Go for a range of sizes – they often fit inside each other for easy storage.

MEASURING JUG

I weigh a lot of liquids straight into the bowl for accuracy, but it is useful to be able to pour batters into pans or sauces over desserts, so I'd recommend investing in one.

SCALES

A reliable pair of good-quality digital scales will completely change your life in baking. Baking is a science that requires accuracy to obtain fantastic results, so a bad set will limit you greatly. Invest in a reputable brand as they are less likely to go wrong and will last for a long time.

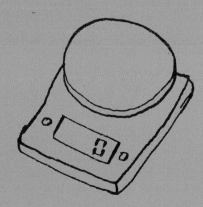

ELECTRIC HAND-HELD WHISK/STAND MIXER

If you are new to baking, I'd really recommend purchasing an electric hand-held whisk. It will make cake-making so much quicker, and is necessary for some tasks like whipping egg whites. They aren't too expensive online and are essential if you want to progress in baking. If you bake a lot, a stand mixer such as a KitchenAid or Kenwood kMix will revolutionise the way you bake. Everything becomes super-fast; I use mine most days. They are costly, but I don't regret it for a minute.

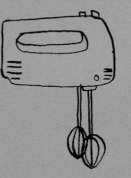

FOOD PROCESSOR OR STICK BLENDER

A food processor is a great thing to own for ease, and I find it most useful for making pastry quickly. A stick blender is a cheaper alternative – great for puréeing fruits and crushing nuts in the blender attachment many brands now include.

ICE-CREAM SCOOP

I use ice-cream scoops for so much more than scooping ice-cream. In fact, it is probably one of my most used pieces of kitchen equipment. I have 3 sizes, and they are ideal for baking even-sized cupcakes, perfectly circular cookies and even distributing batters between cake tins.

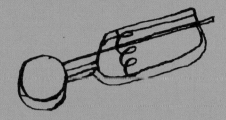

PALETTE KNIFE

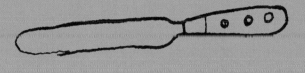

To get a beautiful, smooth finish on cakes, you will need a palette knife. I have a larger one for smoothing the edges of my cakes, and then a mini offset knife for adding detail to cupcakes and the top of cakes.

DOUGH SCRAPER

As well as being useful for handling wet doughs, a dough scraper is a lifesaver for cleaning worktops quickly! I'd purchase one for this reason alone.

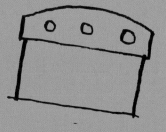

SUGAR THERMOMETER

If you want to extend your baking repertoire to more challenging things like sweet making, caramels and chocolate work, a thermometer will make recipes failsafe and easier to follow. You'll get better results than trying to measure by eye.

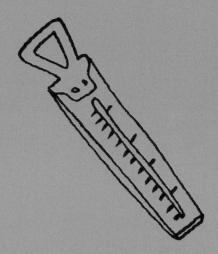

PIPING BAG AND NOZZLES

I always use disposable piping bags, and if you've ever attempted to clean a cloth bag you'll understand why! The only nozzles I use are Wilton – in particular the 1D closed star. This is perfect for icing cupcakes and larger cakes beautifully.

Wooden spoons, spatulas, measuring spoons, a hand whisk, sharp knives and other basic items are all obviously useful in baking and found in most kitchens.

INGREDIENTS

FLOUR

Flour is one of the most important ingredients you will buy. I use plain flour in most of my recipes instead of self-raising, because I like to control the amount of raising agent I am adding. For bread, I always use strong plain flour because it contains a higher level of gluten, which is important in the structure of the dough.

SUGAR

Caster sugar is the most common sugar used in this book as it is so versatile. It makes up the base of most cakes, biscuits, meringues and caramels. Brown sugars, for example muscovado, have a richer, more caramel-like flavour and are suited to stickier cakes. You can substitute any recipes specifying caster sugar with golden caster sugar.

EGGS

I use free-range large eggs in all my recipes, so to get exactly the same results this is what I recommend. Saying that, I do use mixed sizes when it is all I have left and I've never encountered many problems. Keep your eggs at room temperature to make them easier to mix into batters.

BUTTER

A lot of bakers use unsalted butter in recipes, but I have never had any issues using salted butter and then removing the salt from recipes I have used in the past. I like the rich butteriness salted butter gives biscuits and cakes. Unsalted butter is only essential in buttercreams, where too much salt is undesirable.

YEAST

I always use instant yeast. You can add it straight to flour without needing to activate it in water, so it is the easiest to use. Make sure your yeast is in date, or it won't work and your bread won't rise.

FOOD COLOURING

Gel food colourings are more effective than liquid ones. They produce a stronger colour and you only need to add a tiny amount to get the desired shade. This means the colouring lasts longer and doesn't affect the consistency of the batter.

CHOCOLATE AND COCOA POWDER

Quality is key here, as using cheap chocolate or chocolate alternatives can dramatically alter your bakes – 70% dark chocolate is my favourite and I always try to use Fairtrade chocolate and cocoa whenever I can.

JAMS

Making your own jam is a fantastic way of getting a lovely fruitiness into all manner of bakes.

And, by preserving seasonal fruit at their best, you can lock in their fresh flavours, adding others to complement the fruit. The general ratio for the weight of sugar to fruit is 1:1. If you want the jam to be sharper, you can reduce the sugar as I have done in the raspberry jam recipe opposite.

The secret to a well-set jam lies in a substance called pectin, which is present in all fruits. Combined with sugar and acid, pectin will gel, which thickens the jam, then adding lemon juice acidifies the mixture, allowing the pectin to work more effectively. Using jam sugar is not essential, but it does contain extra pectin, which will help ensure success!

Extra flavourings can either be added to the fruit at the start (this works well with dry spices like cinnamon sticks) or stirred into the hot jam after it has been boiled (this works best with liquid flavourings like rosewater or other extracts).

SPICED BLACKBERRY JAM

350g blackberries

350g granulated or jam sugar

Juice of ½ a lemon

1 star anise

1 cinnamon stick

RASPBERRY AND ALMOND JAM

350g raspberries

250g granulated or jam sugar

Juice of ½ a lemon

1 tsp almond extract

APRICOT, PEACH AND VANILLA JAM

200g apricots, stoned and quartered

2 large peaches, stoned and chopped into small pieces

250g granulated or jam sugar

Juice of ½ a lemon

1 tsp vanilla bean paste

MAKES ONE LARGE JAR OR TWO SMALLER JARS

You will also need one large 500g jar or two smaller 250g jars with lids.

1. Put a small saucer into the fridge to chill. This is to test the jam later.

2. Sterilise the jars and lids: wash them thoroughly with hot soapy water, rinse then dry them completely in an oven preheated to 110°C/90 °C fan/gas ¼.

3. Combine the fruit, sugar, lemon juice and any dry flavourings in a large, heavy-based saucepan. The mixture will bubble up so make sure the pan is quite deep. Heat on medium, stirring all the time, until the sugar has dissolved completely.

4. When you can no longer see any sugar granules, turn the heat up and allow the mixture to boil for 5–7 minutes. To test if the jam is ready, spoon a small amount of jam onto the chilled saucer and leave to set for 30 seconds. When you push the jam with your finger, it should have formed a skin that ripples slightly. If it doesn't, continue to boil and test again a few minutes later.

5. When the jam is ready, remove any spices and stir in any liquid flavourings like almond extract then carefully spoon it into the sterilised jars. Use a funnel if you have one. Fill the jars to the top then put the lids on. Jam will keep for months in a cool dark place but store in the fridge once opened.

CURDS

Curds are what I call flavour injectors. You only need a small amount to make a real impact.

They can elevate the simplest bakes to far more delicious levels. Use them to sandwich together a vanilla sponge, fill warm doughnuts or make your macarons pack a punch. Their complexity is all about the balance of acidity and sugar – a great curd should have an intense flavour that showcases fruity flavours without being overly sweet. People often think curds are limited to just lemon, or at least citrus fruits, but you can actually use any acidic fruit juices like raspberry or cranberry. Just substitute 150ml of your favourite juice in the recipes opposite to create any curd you like. My method is so simple: all the ingredients go into one pan and are heated gently until the mixture thickens.

Eggs give curds their luxurious and creamy feel: when the mixture is heated the eggs emulsify, which makes the curd set firmly. It is important to keep the mixture moving as it heats, so the eggs set properly and the curd is smooth. For the first five minutes, the curd won't change very much so whisking it seems pointless. However, once the mixture reaches the correct temperature, it will thicken immediately. The change happens rapidly, so keep an eye on it while heating it.

 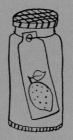 

PASSIONFRUIT CURD

LEMON OR LIME CURD

RASPBERRY CURD

10 passionfruit, halved and
flesh scooped out of the
skins
100g unsalted butter
150g caster sugar
2 eggs plus 2 yolks

Zest and juice of 4 unwaxed
lemons or limes
100g unsalted butter
150g caster sugar
2 eggs plus 2 yolks

150g raspberries
Zest and juice of 2 unwaxed
lemons
100g unsalted butter
150g caster sugar
2 eggs plus 2 yolks

MAKES TWO SMALL JARS

You will also need 2 sterilised jars and lids to store the curd.

1. Sterilise the jars and lids you are using (see instructions on page 19) and
   put to one side.
2. Briefly whizz any seeded fruits, if using (for example raspberries or
   passionfruit), in a food processor to loosen the seeds from the juice.
   Strain the liquid through a sieve into a jug – this will be your fruit juice.
   If you want a curd with seeds in it (passionfruit seeds are particularly
   nice), stir a few tablespoons of the leftover pulp into the curd before
   you pour it into the jars.
3. In a medium saucepan, combine the juice with all the other ingredients.
   Heat on low, whisking all the time, until the butter has completely melted.
4. Turn the heat up to medium and continue to whisk. After 5–6 minutes,
   the mixture will thicken enough to coat the back of a spoon. Remove
   from the heat, pour into the sterilised jars and screw on the lids. The curd
   will keep in the fridge for up to two weeks.

LITTLE
CAKES

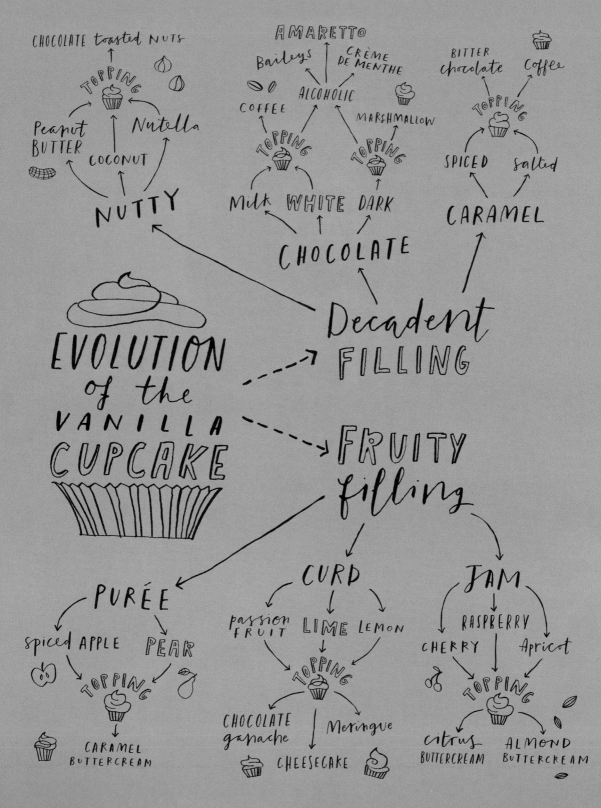

CHOCOLATE toasted NUTS

TOPPING

Peanut BUTTER Nutella

COCONUT

NUTTY

AMARETTO

Baileys CRÈME DE MENTHE

ALCOHOLIC

COFFEE MARSHMALLOW

TOPPING TOPPING

Milk WHITE DARK

CHOCOLATE

BITTER chocolate Coffee

TOPPING

SPICED Salted

CARAMEL

EVOLUTION of the VANILLA CUPCAKE

Decadent FILLING

FRUITY filling

PURÉE

Spiced APPLE PEAR

TOPPING

CARAMEL BUTTERCREAM

CURD

passion FRUIT LIME LEMON

TOPPING

CHOCOLATE ganache Meringue

CHEESECAKE

JAM

RASPBERRY

CHERRY Apricot

TOPPING

citrus BUTTERCREAM ALMOND BUTTERCREAM

CUPCAKES

A few years ago, the world went cupcake crazy.

Fairy cakes and butterfly cakes, lovingly assembled with modest amounts of buttercream, runny icing and jelly diamonds, were banished from our kitchens in favour of their colourful American cousin.

Now commonplace in bakeries and supermarkets alike, the humble cupcake has earned itself a bad reputation for being dry and sickly sweet, something I don't believe they should be. Correctly done, they have the potential to be something truly wonderful.

Balancing flavours is the first place to start. Sweet toppings like buttercream or meringue need a sharp filling to offset the sugary nature of the cake, and rich caramel or chocolate need a bitter accompaniment like coffee or alcohol, to make them palatable. Take a look at the cupcake evolution tree opposite to see how I go about matching complementary flavours in my baking, and then try experimenting with new flavours of your own!

MY FAVOURITE VANILLA CUPCAKES

To make these cakes, I use the reverse creaming method, as opposed to the more common creaming method. Instead of beating air into the sugar and butter, adding the eggs then stirring in the dry ingredients, the reverse creaming method requires the butter to be rubbed into the dry ingredients, followed by milk and eggs. As well as being simpler, with fewer stages, I think this method produces a better textured, more even sponge. When you rub the butter into the flour and sugar, the flour particles get coated in fat, which minimises gluten formation in the cake. Gluten is the essential component in bread, but in cakes too much can produce a tough and chewy sponge.

MAKES 12

175g plain flour
200g caster sugar
75g butter
1½ tsp baking powder
2 eggs, at room temperature
90ml whole milk, at room temperature
1 tsp vanilla bean paste

You will also need a stand mixer, 12-hole cupcake tin and paper cupcake cases.

1. Preheat the oven to 180°C/160°C fan/gas 4. Line the cupcake tin with 12 cupcake cases. In the bowl of a stand mixer, combine the flour, sugar, butter and baking powder using the paddle attachment. Mix on a low speed until the mixture resembles fine breadcrumbs. You shouldn't see any large lumps of butter. Alternatively, use your fingers to rub the butter into the flour and sugar.

2. In a small jug, use a fork to blend the eggs, milk and vanilla bean paste together. Add the mixture a little at a time to the bowl, beating until it is all combined. Keep beating for a few minutes more, until the mixture is uniform and smooth with no lumps.

3. Divide the mixture between the cases evenly, filling each one no more than two-thirds full. Bake in the preheated oven for 16–18 minutes, until a skewer inserted comes out clean and the cakes are a pale golden brown. Don't be tempted to over-bake here; get them out as soon as the skewer is clean. The last thing you want is dry cakes!

4. Leave to cool for five minutes in the tin, then remove and leave to cool completely on a cooling rack. Do not attempt to core, fill or decorate them until they are cold.

LEMON CHEESECAKE CUPCAKES

With their unusual cheesecake topping, which works really well with the tangy lemon curd, these cupcakes make a great dessert.

MAKES 12

1 x My Favourite Vanilla
    Cupcakes recipe
    (page 26)
Zest of 1 unwaxed lemon

FILLING
12 tsp lemon curd
    (see recipe page 21)

ICING
100g full-fat cream cheese
350g icing sugar
150ml double cream

TOPPING
50g digestive biscuits
1 tsp butter, melted

1. Make My Favourite Vanilla Cupcakes recipe, adding the lemon zest to the batter at the same time as the eggs and milk. Make sure they are completely cold before decorating them.

2. To make the icing, put the cream cheese into a large bowl, and use an electric hand-held whisk to beat it until smooth. Add the icing sugar, a few tablespoons at a time, until it is all incorporated. Mix in the double cream and whisk until the mixture thickens. You can whisk this by hand, but it will take a few more minutes to thicken. It won't hold its shape yet, so it is important to chill it in the fridge for at least an hour so that it firms up.

3. Put the biscuits for the topping in a sealable plastic bag, seal it and then, using a rolling pin, lightly bash the bag to crush the biscuits into small pieces.

4. Add the biscuit crumbs to the melted butter and stir until the mixture starts to clump together.

5. To assemble, use a sharp knife or specialist cupcake corer to make a circular incision in the centre of each cupcake. Take out the middle and fill each cavity with ½ teaspoon of lemon curd.

6. When the icing has set, put it into a disposable piping bag. Cut the end off the bag, making a medium-sized circular hole, then pipe a double ring around the edge of the lemon curd, and fill the gap with the remaining lemon curd.

7. Sprinkle the topping around the icing ring, trying to avoid the lemon curd centre. These cupcakes need to be stored in the fridge, where they will keep for up to three days.

CARAMEL MACCHIATO CUPCAKES

Pairing bitter coffee with a sweet salted caramel sauce makes for mellow, not overly sweet, cupcakes. You can add more coffee to the icing if you prefer a stronger flavour.

MAKES 12

1 x My Favourite Vanilla
  Cupcakes recipe
  (page 26)
2 tsp instant coffee
  granules, dissolved in
  2 tbsp of boiling water

COFFEE BUTTERCREAM

75g unsalted butter,
  softened
250g icing sugar
2 tbsp milk
3 tsp instant coffee
  granules, dissolved in
  2 tbsp of boiling water

CARAMEL FILLING

200g caster sugar
25g butter
50ml double cream
Pinch of sea salt

1. Make My Favourite Vanilla Cupcakes recipe, adding the coffee into the mixture at the same time as the eggs and milk. Leave to cool completely before decorating.

2. To make the coffee buttercream, put the soft butter into a large bowl or into the bowl of a stand mixer and beat for a minute or so. It's really important that the butter is soft enough to mix evenly with the icing sugar.

3. Add the icing sugar, milk and coffee and continue to beat for 5–10 minutes, until the icing is light and fluffy. You want a consistency that just falls off the spoon but holds its shape when dropped. If the icing is looking too runny or too thick, add a few tablespoons of icing sugar or a dash more milk.

4. To make the caramel filling, put the caster sugar into a large, heavy-based saucepan. Add 4 tablespoons of water and stir over a low heat until the sugar and water are well mixed and the sugar has dissolved. Turn the heat up and allow to boil until the mixture starts to caramelise. Don't stir at this point or the sugar will crystallise and you will have to start again! You want the caramel to be a light amber colour (reading about 165°C on a sugar thermometer if you have one).

5. As soon as it reaches the desired colour, take the pan off the heat and stir in the butter. It will splutter and spit, so be careful. Once smooth, add the cream and sea salt and mix until glossy. Leave to cool completely before using. This filling can be made in advance and stored in a sealed container in the fridge for up to two weeks.

6. To assemble, core each cupcake using a sharp knife or specialist cupcake corer, then fill the centres with most of the caramel filling, reserving a little for the tops.

7. Next, use a small palette knife to spread the coffee buttercream over the top of each cake. You could pipe it on, but I like to smooth it out, to make the cakes look like the top of a mug of coffee.

8. Transfer the remaining caramel filling to a disposable piping bag. Cut the end off the bag, making a small circular hole, and pipe a mesh-like pattern over the top of each cake, just like a macchiato coffee.

TOASTED MARSHMALLOW CUPCAKES

I love the smoky flavour and crisp outer shell of a slightly singed marshmallow that's been toasted over a bonfire. I've balanced the sweetness of the sticky topping by filling the cupcakes with a bitter chocolate ganache.

MAKES 12

60g digestive biscuits
(about 4)
1 x My Favourite Vanilla
Cupcakes recipe
(page 26)

GANACHE FILLING
100g dark chocolate
(70–80% cocoa solids)
1 tsp butter
50ml double cream

MARSHMALLOW TOPPING
125g caster sugar
75g golden syrup
2 large egg whites
½ tsp vanilla extract
4 squares of dark chocolate,
to decorate

You will also need an electric hand-held whisk.

1. Blitz the digestive biscuits in a food processor until they are finely ground, or put them into a sealable bag, seal the bag and crush with a rolling pin. There shouldn't be any large pieces remaining.

2. Make My Favourite Vanilla Cupcakes recipe, adding the digestive biscuit crumbs with the flour in step 1.

3. To make the filling, finely chop the chocolate and put it into a small bowl. Heat the butter and cream in a saucepan until steaming hot but not boiling, then pour over the chocolate. Remove from the heat and leave to stand for a minute before stirring to form a smooth ganache. If any lumps of chocolate remain, put the bowl into the microwave for ten seconds then stir; repeat until the lumps are gone. Chill in the fridge for 30 minutes or so, until it is firm and scoopable.

4. To make the marshmallow topping, put the sugar, golden syrup and 2 tablespoons of water into a saucepan and cook over a medium-high heat without stirring until the mixture reaches the soft-ball stage (118°C on a sugar thermometer). If you don't have a thermometer, the mixture is ready when the bubbles start to stick together in the pan and it drips off a spoon in a steady stream. Remove from the heat.

5. Put the egg whites into a clean, grease-free bowl and whisk with an electric hand-held whisk until soft peaks form. With the whisk on low, carefully pour the hot sugar onto the egg whites, whisking all the time. When all the sugar has been added, increase the speed to high and whip until the sides of the bowl feel only slightly warm and the mixture is thick and glossy. Add the vanilla extract at the end. This icing is easiest to pipe when it is warm, so transfer immediately to a piping bag fitted with a large circular nozzle or with the tip cut off.

6. To assemble, use a sharp knife or specialist cupcake corer to make a circular incision in the centre of each cupcake, remove the centre and fill each one with a teaspoon of the chocolate filling.

7. Pipe a large mound of marshmallow topping on the top of each cupcake, covering the chocolate filling. Use a blowtorch, if you have one, to lightly brown each one, avoiding the paper case as this will burn. You could use the grill to brown the marshmallow topping, but watch carefully because it is more difficult to control the colour and prevent it burning.

8. To finish, chop the chocolate squares finely and sprinkle over the top of the marshmallow.

NEVER-FAIL CHOCOLATE CUPCAKES

I always think that good chocolate cake is the mark of a great baker. Here, using oil instead of butter gives the sponge a soft and tender texture, and helps keep it moist. Oil can't trap air in the same way as butter, because the fat is in liquid form, so the raising agents provide the lift instead. This recipe yields beautifully moist, cocoa-rich cupcakes that are incredibly quick and work every time.

MAKES 12

175g caster sugar
60ml sunflower oil (any unflavoured oil will do)
1 egg
1 tsp vanilla extract
100g plain flour
35g cocoa powder
½ tsp bicarbonate of soda
½ tsp baking powder
¼ tsp salt
150ml strong coffee, cooled (or water)

CHOCOLATE GANACHE
200g butter
275g dark chocolate (60–70% cocoa solids), chopped
2 tbsp golden syrup
250ml double cream

You will also need a 12-hole muffin tin and 12 paper cases.

1. Preheat the oven to 180°C/160°C fan/gas 4 and line the muffin tin with paper cases.

2. Use a whisk to combine the sugar, oil and egg in a large bowl until smooth. Add the vanilla and whisk again.

3. Sift the flour, cocoa powder, bicarbonate of soda, baking powder and salt together in a separate bowl.

4. Add a third of the flour mixture to the egg mixture, followed by half the coffee, beating well after each addition. Repeat until all the flour and coffee are incorporated. The batter will be quite liquid, but that's fine.

5. Divide the mixture evenly between the cases, filling each one two-thirds full. Put into the preheated oven and bake for 20–25 minutes, until springy to the touch and a skewer inserted comes out clean. Leave to cool completely before decorating.

6. To make the ganache, put the butter, chocolate and golden syrup into a heatproof bowl over a pan of simmering water. Stir for 7–8 minutes until the mixture is melted and smooth. Pour in the double cream and mix until combined.

7. To make shiny, smooth-topped cupcakes, use a sharp knife to level off the cupcakes, if necessary, then pour the warm ganache onto the cool cupcakes and leave to set at room temperature. If you want to make a pipeable topping, put the ganache into the fridge for 35–40 minutes and chill until cool, but not set. Use an electric hand-held whisk to whip the ganache for 2–3 minutes, until it turns from dark to pale brown. Transfer to a piping bag fitted with a closed star nozzle and pipe swirls on the top of the cakes.

MY FAVOURITE MADELEINES

When I first came across these shell-shaped cakes, I didn't think they were anything special. I could not have been more wrong! They are light as air, perfect for dipping in a multitude of hot drinks, and I guarantee you'll be wishing the pan made more than 12 at a time! A simple glaze is all you need to show them off in all their glory; it should harden slightly so it cracks when you eat it, keeping the inside moist. Madeleines are best served as fresh as possible.

MAKES 12

100g caster sugar
2 eggs
100g plain flour
½ tsp baking powder
1 tsp vanilla bean paste
100g butter, melted, plus
    extra for greasing

GLAZE
125g icing sugar
2 tbsp milk
1 tsp vanilla bean paste

You will also need a stand mixer or an electric hand-held whisk and a 12-hole madeleine tin. You could use a mini muffin tin but you won't get the characteristic shape.

1. Put the sugar and eggs into the bowl of a stand mixer and whisk at high speed until the mixture is light and thick, around 6–7 minutes. Alternatively, you can do this in a bowl with an electric hand-held whisk but it will take a little longer. To check that enough air has been incorporated, take the whisk out and if it leaves a trail that takes three seconds to disappear back into the original mixture, it's ready.

2. Combine the flour and baking powder in a small bowl, then sift over the egg mixture. Using a metal spoon or a flexible spatula, fold in the dry ingredients until all the flour is mixed in.

3. Stir the vanilla into the melted butter, then add a little bit at a time to the batter, stirring to combine. At this stage, the mixture will be fairly runny. Chill it in the fridge for at least 30 minutes to rest and firm up.

4. Grease a madeleine tin liberally with butter (I use my fingers to make sure all the crevices are covered) and put into the freezer to chill. Preheat the oven to 200°C/180°C fan/gas 6.

5. Spoon one heaped teaspoon of batter into each mould. The mixture will spread out as it bakes, so don't try to fill the mould. Bake for 8–10 minutes, until the middle has risen into the classic dome shape and they are golden brown.

6. To make the glaze, put the icing sugar into a small bowl and stir briefly to break up any large lumps of sugar. Add the milk and vanilla bean paste and beat well. You should get a loose mixture that does not hold its shape when dripped into the bowl. If it seems too thick, add a little more milk.

7. Dip the warm madeleines into the glaze using your hands, making sure they are fully coated. Allow the excess to drip back into the bowl, then put onto a cooling rack to harden (I put a baking tray underneath to catch the drips).

NEAPOLITAN MADELEINES

Madeleines are shell-shaped, so as a play on their seaside roots I've created my own take on Neapolitan ice-cream, using vanilla sponge, freeze-dried strawberries and rich dark chocolate.

MAKES 12

1 x My Favourite
  Madeleines recipe
  (page 35)

CHOCOLATE GLAZE
3 tbsp butter
100g dark chocolate,
  chopped
A sprinkle of freeze-dried
  strawberries
Hundreds and thousands
  (optional)

1. Make My Favourite Madeleines recipe but don't glaze them. Leave them to cool.
2. Melt the butter and chocolate together in a heatproof bowl over a pan of simmering water.
3. Dip the madeleines into the chocolate so they are half-covered.
4. Immediately sprinkle the chocolate with strawberry pieces or dip into sprinkles for a more child-friendly version. Leave to set at room temperature on a piece of baking parchment.

RASPBERRY AND PISTACHIO FRIANDS

These little cakes remind me of a more sophisticated, stripped-back cupcake. Full of flavour with a dense but chewy crumb, it's like frangipane meets fairy cake. Beautifully simple to make, the biggest pitfall is not greasing your tins properly. If you don't have non-stick muffin tins or friand tins, make sure you butter them to death or you'll have eight fabulous cakes that you can't get out of the tins...

MAKES 8

200g butter, plus extra for greasing
100g pistachio nuts, plus a few extra to serve
200g icing sugar
85g ground almonds
85g plain flour
5 large egg whites
1 small punnet of raspberries
Icing sugar, to dust (optional)

You will also need an 8- or 12-hole muffin or friand tin and a food processor.

1. Preheat the oven to 180°C/160°C fan/gas 4. Melt the butter in a small pan, then remove from the heat and leave to cool a little. Grease eight holes of the friand (or muffin) tin with a little bit of butter.

2. Blitz 85g of the pistachio nuts in a food processor with the icing sugar until very finely chopped. Tip into a bowl with the ground almonds and flour and mix together. Roughly chop the remaining pistachio nuts and set aside.

3. Froth the egg whites lightly with a fork, then pour into the nuts and flour mixture with the melted butter and mix well.

4. Pour the mixture into the friand tin holes, add a few raspberries to each one, then scatter with the chopped pistachios. Bake for 20–25 minutes until the friands are risen and springy to the touch and a skewer inserted comes out clean.

5. Serve warm or at room temperature. Dust with a little icing sugar if you like. They should be light and chewy!

TWIST: PECAN PIE FRIANDS

Make the friand recipe above, swapping pistachios for 100g pecan nuts and the raspberries for 75g chewy toffee, chopped into small pieces. Sprinkle the toffee over the friand batter before baking.

MUFFINS

When making homemade muffins, it is always a struggle to create the lofty domed top you find on the professional ones in coffee shops and supermarkets.

Too often they come out of the oven looking small and flat, but this recipe should help!

To get muffins with a great rise, you need to fill the cases right to the top. A hot oven is also essential to generate enough steam to get the initial lift in the muffins but high heat can also cause excess browning and a crunchy, thick top which stops the muffins rising. To prevent this, I use steam: I fill some of the muffin tin holes with water, the water evaporates creating steam, which stops the outside of the muffins browning too quickly and gives them time to rise fully before a crust forms. A similar technique is used with bread to stop the crust forming before the dough has fully expanded.

The secret to tender muffins lies in the mixing. Be careful when folding the ingredients together, because pouring wet ingredients onto flour that hasn't been coated in fat screams gluten development. The more you mix the batter, the stronger the gluten becomes and the tougher the muffins will be. If you want to see the effect of overmixing, keep a little bit of the mixture back and stir it for a few extra minutes. Bake in the same way as the rest, and you will notice it won't rise in the same way and the inside will be full of tunnels of air rather than small bubbles.

MY FAVOURITE MUFFINS

MAKES 8

225g plain flour
1½ tsp baking powder
¼ tsp bicarbonate of soda
100g caster sugar
75g butter
180g yoghurt
40ml whole milk
1 egg

You will also need a 12-hole muffin tin and eight paper cases.

1. In a large bowl, combine the plain flour, baking powder, bicarbonate of soda and caster sugar and mix well so the raising agents are evenly dispersed through the dry mix.

2. Melt the butter in a small pan on the hob or in a small jug in the microwave, then whisk in the yoghurt and milk followed by the egg. It is important to mix the ingredients in this order to avoid the hot butter cooking the egg.

3. Pour the wet mixture over the dry mixture, and use a rubber spatula to fold together. Mix until just combined, scooping the flour from underneath to avoid any large, dry patches. This is the crucial stage in muffin-making; you want to mix until the wet and dry ingredients are just combined. Overmixing will result in a tough, chewy cake. The mixture will be quite thick, but this helps achieve a perfectly domed muffin.

4. Chill the batter for at least 30 minutes. This is not essential if you're in a hurry, but it allows the flour to hydrate and relaxes the gluten developed during the mixing, which results in a softer cake. You can also leave the batter overnight and it will still produce great muffins.

5. Preheat the oven to 200°C/180°C fan/gas 6 and line the muffin tin with eight paper cases. Use a tablespoon to divide the mixture between the cases and fill them nearly to the top. The thickness of the mixture means it rises upwards into a beautiful dome, rather than spilling over the edges.

6. Fill the remaining four holes in the muffin tin with boiling water. This creates steam in the oven, which stops a tough crust forming on the muffins.

7. Bake at 200°C/180°C fan/gas 6 for five minutes, then reduce the oven temperature to 170°C/150°C fan/gas 3 and bake for a further 10–15 minutes, until a skewer inserted comes out clean.

DOUBLE CHOCOLATE CHIP MUFFINS

Use whatever variety of chocolate you prefer – I like the combination of white and dark chocolate.

MAKES 8

1 x My Favourite Muffins
    recipe (page 41)
70g white chocolate,
    chopped
70g dark chocolate,
    chopped

1. Make My Favourite Muffins recipe up to step 4.

2. After each teaspoon of batter is spooned into the muffin cases, press a few chocolate chunks into the batter. This helps get an even distribution of chocolate throughout the muffin and stops large chunks getting stuck at the bottom.

3. Bake as on page 41, then eat when warm to get the full melted chocolate experience!

LEMON AND POPPY SEED MUFFINS

I think lemon and poppy seeds are a winning combination in big, light muffins. The tiny black specks give added texture and a beautiful earthy tone, while the zingy lemon glaze makes these into crowd-pleasers.

MAKES 8

1 x My Favourite Muffins
    recipe (page 41)
Zest of 1 unwaxed lemon
3 tbsp poppy seeds

GLAZE
150g icing sugar
Juice from ½ a lemon

1. Make My Favourite Muffins recipe up to step 4, adding the lemon zest and poppy seeds to the dry mix in step 1.

2. Bake as on page 41, then remove from the oven and leave to cool in the tin while you make the glaze.

3. Sift the icing sugar into a small bowl, then add the lemon juice little by little to make a paste that is just thin enough to drip off the spoon in a steady stream. Dip the warm cakes top down into the runny glaze and leave to set before enjoying.

BREAKFAST MUFFINS

These muffins make a great breakfast that you can take with you to work or school, or enjoy at home with your morning coffee. They are so quick to make that you could even prep the batter the night before you want to bake, store it in the fridge overnight then cook them in the morning.

MAKES 8

1 x My Favourite Muffins
  recipe (page 41),
100g wholemeal flour
100g fresh or frozen
  raspberries
2 tsp chia seeds
50g of your favourite
  granola or crunchy cereal
  (I use Crunchy Nut
  cornflakes)
2 tbsp runny honey

1. Make My Favourite Muffins recipe up to step 4 but replace 100g of plain flour with 100g of wholemeal flour.

2. After each teaspoon of batter is spooned into the muffin cases, press a few torn raspberries into it. Once the cases are full, sprinkle the chia seeds and cereal over the top of the muffins, covering the whole surface.

3. Bake as on page 41. If the topping starts to catch, cover the muffins with tin foil to stop them burning.

4. Drizzle the warm cakes with honey, then enjoy hot or cold as a portable breakfast treat.

CAKES

Malted milk

18cm PIÑATA CAKE

PERFECT FOR PARTIES

CHERRY AND DARK CHOCOLATE

Apricot pistachio and honey

UPSIDE-DOWN CAKE

FAVOURITE VANILLA CAKE RECIPE

x3

x2

BEAUTIFUL NATURAL INGREDIENTS

GIN AND TONIC

GREAT FOR CELEBRATIONS

x3

x2

DRIZZLE CAKE

18cm LAYER CAKE

CARAMEL NUT BRITTLE CAKE

EVERYDAY CLASSIC WITH A TWIST

Pink grapefruit

MY FAVOURITE VANILLA CAKE

Having a staple vanilla cake recipe that is moist, moreish and works every time is essential to every great baker. I've put together a basic recipe that makes one layer of cake, ready to be used as a canvas for exotic flavours and fantastic creations.

I find baking individual layers for cakes easier than slicing one large cake into layers, but it is important that the individual sponges rise evenly so they stack well. Oven temperature is the key to success here. An oven set too hot will cause the outside of the cake to set before the inside has finished expanding. This results in a domed, cracked sponge that is difficult to stack. An oven set too low will make the batter set too slowly which results in a dense, heavy cake due to gas bubbles not being able to expand properly. For a single 20cm thin sponge, a temperature of 170°C/150°C fan/gas 3 gives a great even rise without doming. For a larger or deeper cake, a slightly lower temperature of 160°C/140°C fan/gas 3 allows the inside to fully cook without the top turning too crispy.

MAKES ONE 18cm CAKE

40g unsalted butter, plus extra for greasing
125g caster sugar
100g plain flour
1 tsp baking powder
⅛ tsp salt
100ml whole milk
1 egg
1 tsp vanilla extract

You will also need an 18cm tin and a stand mixer or an electric hand-held whisk.

1. Preheat the oven to 170°C/150°C fan/gas 3. Grease an 18cm tin and line with baking parchment.
2. Put the butter, sugar, flour, baking powder and salt into the bowl of a stand mixer fitted with a paddle attachment. Mix on low until all the butter is rubbed into the dry mixture and it has a sandy texture. To do this by hand, rub the butter into the dry ingredients as if you were making pastry.
3. In a small jug, beat together the milk, egg and vanilla. Pour the mixture down the side of the bowl containing the dry ingredients and beat until everything is mixed together. When all the liquid has been added, beat on a high speed for two minutes until it is really well combined and smooth. If doing this by hand, use an electric hand-held whisk.
4. Pour the mixture into the prepared tin and bake in the preheated oven for 25–30 minutes until golden brown or a skewer inserted comes out clean.

PINK GRAPEFRUIT DRIZZLE CAKE

Lemon drizzle cake is my mum's absolute favourite cake – she loves the crunch of the sugar and the acidic lemon tang cutting through the sweetness. Here, I have modernised this classic, giving it an update with pink grapefruit or gin and tonic toppings, but if you want to keep it simple you could still use lemon.

SERVES 10–12

Butter, for greasing
2 x My Favourite Vanilla
    Cake recipe (page 47)
Zest of 1 pink grapefruit

DRIZZLE
150g granulated sugar
Juice of ½ a pink grapefruit

You will also need a 1kg loaf tin.

1. Preheat the oven to 180°C/160°C fan/gas 4. Grease a loaf tin and line with a long strip of baking parchment down the middle that hangs over the sides – this will make the cake easier to remove from the tin.

2. Make two batches of My Favourite Vanilla Cake recipe up to step 3. Fold most of the grapefruit zest into the batter, reserving a little for the top.

3. Pour into the tin and bake for 40–45 minutes until risen, springy, and a skewer inserted comes out clean.

4. For the drizzle, mix the sugar and grapefruit juice together. Pour over the hot cake and leave to cool. The zesty juices will soak through the cake and you'll be left with the classic crunchy top. Sprinkle over the remaining grapefruit zest before serving.

TWIST: GIN AND TONIC DRIZZLE CAKE

Replace the grapefruit zest with the zest of half an unwaxed lime, then bake in the same way as specified above. Swap the grapefruit juice in the drizzle with 25ml gin, one tablespoon of tonic water and two tablespoons of lime juice and drizzle over the cooked cake. Sprinkle with the zest of the remaining half a lime before serving.

CARAMEL NUT BRITTLE LAYER CAKE

Nut brittles are so delicious, but often they are merely the supporting act or final flourish, never allowed to be the main event. This cake showcases shards of light-catching mixed nut brittle as well as a crumbly praline, and it is every bit as tasty as it looks. I use My Favourite Vanilla Cake recipe, swapping some of the sugar for soft brown instead of caster, which gives the sponge a subtle caramel flavour that goes with the rest of the cake.

SERVES 12

120g unsalted butter, cubed, plus extra for greasing
125g caster sugar
250g soft light brown sugar
300g plain flour
3 tsp baking powder
½ tsp salt
300ml whole milk
3 eggs
1 tsp vanilla bean paste

ALMOND SYRUP
70g caster sugar
½ tsp almond extract
25ml almond liqueur (optional)

BUTTERCREAM
200g unsalted butter, softened
400g icing sugar
2 tbsp milk
1 tsp vanilla bean paste
½ tsp almond extract (optional)

1. Grease three 18cm tins and line with baking parchment and preheat the oven to 180°C/160°C fan/gas 4. I use smaller tins for this recipe to give extra height so the assembled cake looks more impressive.

2. To make the cake, put the sugars, flour, baking powder and salt into the bowl of a stand mixer fitted with the paddle attachment. Use your fingers to break up any large lumps of brown sugar that you see in the mixture. Add the butter in cubes, and then mix on low until it is rubbed into the dry mixture and it has a sandy texture. Alternatively, rub the butter into the dry ingredients by hand, as if you were making pastry.

3. In a small jug, beat together the milk, eggs and vanilla. Pour the mixture down the side of the bowl with the dry ingredients and beat until everything is mixed together. When all the liquid has been added, beat on a high speed for two minutes until it is really well combined and smooth. Alternatively, use an electric hand-held whisk. Divide the mixture evenly between the prepared tins and bake in the preheated oven for 25–30 minutes until golden brown.

4. While the cake is baking, make the almond syrup. Put the sugar into a small saucepan with 50ml of water and bring to the boil. Simmer for two minutes, then remove from the heat. Stir in the almond extract and liqueur, if using. Pour into a jug and allow to cool.

5. Remove the cooked cakes from the oven and leave to cool in their tins for ten minutes. Use a skewer or toothpick to make small holes all over the top of the sponges, then use a pastry brush to liberally cover the cakes in syrup. This helps the sponge to stay moist and injects nutty flavour throughout the whole cake. Leave to cool completely.

BRITTLE
200g roasted nuts of your
    choice, roughly chopped
    (I use a mix of almonds
    and salted peanuts)
300g caster sugar

You will also need three
18cm round tins and a stand
mixer or an electric hand-
held whisk.

6. To make the buttercream, beat the butter in a stand mixer fitted with the paddle attachment, or with an electric hand-held whisk, for a few seconds to soften it further, then add half the icing sugar. Beat on a low speed until all the sugar is combined, then add the remaining sugar, followed by the milk. Turn the mixer up to high speed and beat for at least five minutes, preferably longer, to whip in plenty of air which creates a lighter buttercream. Mix in the vanilla and almond extract (if using) towards the end of the whipping.

7. To make the brittle, line a baking tray with baking parchment. Spread the nuts out evenly over the parchment. Put the sugar into a medium saucepan with 100ml of water. Heat gently over a low heat until all the sugar has dissolved. When you can no longer see grains of sugar, stop stirring immediately and turn up the heat. Allow to boil until the caramel reaches a dark amber colour before removing and pouring over the nuts. Use a palette knife to spread the caramel and nuts out into an even layer then leave to harden.

8. Use a palette knife to spread some of the buttercream onto each cake, then stack the layers on top of each other. Thinly cover the whole cake with a small amount of buttercream. This is called a crumb coat, as it locks in the crumbs and stops them showing on the final cake. Put into the fridge for 30 minutes to harden.

9. Take half of the hard brittle and blitz it in a food processor until it is dusty and in much smaller pieces. Alternatively, you could put the brittle into a sealable plastic bag and bash with a rolling pin to get a similar consistency. Break the rest into shards.

10. Cover the whole chilled cake with the remaining buttercream, using a ruler or large palette knife to achieve a smooth finish on the sides. Press the crumbled brittle around the bottom third of the cake, then arrange the shards on top and sprinkle over smaller pieces of brittle to finish off.

APRICOT, PISTACHIO AND HONEY UPSIDE-DOWN CAKE

Upside-down cakes really bring the magic of baking alive for me. Pouring a thick caramel into the tin first, before adding the fruit, means there is no danger of mushy, overcooked fruit, just jewels enrobed in glossy syrup. Stone fruits work best here, as they keep their shape and look so pretty arranged over the top. I've used My Favourite Vanilla Cake recipe, with added ground pistachio nuts, which keep the sponge tender and give it a great flavour.

SERVES 10

Butter, for greasing
40g pistachio nuts
2 x My Favourite Vanilla
   Cake recipe (page 47)

TOPPING
125g caster sugar
50g runny honey
1 tbsp butter
350g ripe apricots
60g pistachio nuts

You will also need a 20cm round tin and a food processor.

1. Preheat the oven to 180°C/160°C fan/gas 4 and grease and line a 20cm round tin.

2. In a food processor, blitz the pistachio nuts until they are finely ground and no large lumps remain.

3. Make two batches of My Favourite Vanilla Cake recipe, adding the ground pistachio nuts with the flour in step 2.

4. To make the topping, put the sugar and honey into a small saucepan with 50ml of water. Stir over a low heat until all the sugar has dissolved, then turn the heat up to high and simmer without stirring for five minutes, or until the caramel is a golden brown. Add the butter and whisk in quickly. The mixture will bubble and foam violently, so be careful. When you have a smooth caramel, pour it into the tin and tilt the tin to make sure the whole base is covered.

5. Halve and stone the apricots, then put them cut-side down into the caramel. Fill any gaps with pistachio nuts.

6. Pour the cake mixture over the apricots and bake in the preheated oven for 40–50 minutes until golden brown and a skewer inserted comes out clean.

7. Leave to stand for a minute or two, then put a large plate over the top of the tin, turn the tin and plate over, so that the plate is underneath the tin then lift the tin gently away from the cake. The caramel will harden if you leave it too long, so try to do this step within ten minutes of the cake coming out of the oven.

8. Enjoy warm with custard or cream as a dessert, or allow to cool and serve as an afternoon treat.

TWIST: CHOCOLATE AND CHERRY UPSIDE-DOWN CAKE

Swap the apricots for 350g pitted black cherries and mix 100g chopped dark chocolate into the mixture at step 3 instead of the pistachio nuts. Add 25ml cherry kirsch to the saucepan with the water in step 4 instead of the honey.

MALTED MILK PIÑATA CAKE

This is a really fun cake which goes down well with children and adults alike. I use My Favourite Vanilla Cake recipe for this, swapping some of the caster sugar for soft light brown and adding malted milk powder to give the cake a nostalgic, caramelised milk flavour.

SERVES 12

120g butter, plus extra for greasing
125g caster sugar
250g soft light brown sugar
300g plain flour
3 tsp baking powder
2 tbsp Horlicks or other malted milk powder
½ tsp salt
300ml whole milk
3 eggs
1 tsp vanilla bean paste

BUTTERCREAM
50ml whole milk
2 tbsp Horlicks or other malted milk powder
150g unsalted butter, softened
350g icing sugar

FILLING AND DECORATION
Approx 300g milk bottle sweets (ideally the floury kind, they are less sticky)
Coloured paper straws

You will also need three 18cm round tins and a stand mixer or an electric hand-held whisk.

1. Preheat the oven to 180°C/160°C fan/gas 4. Grease three 18cm tins and line with baking parchment.

2. Put the butter, sugars, flour, baking powder, Horlicks and salt into the bowl of a stand mixer fitted with the paddle attachment. Mix on low until all the butter is rubbed into the dry mixture and it has a sandy texture. Alternatively, rub the butter into the dry ingredients by hand, as if you were making pastry.

3. In a small jug, beat together the milk, eggs and vanilla. Pour the mixture down the side of the bowl into the dry ingredients and beat until everything is mixed together. When all the liquid has been added, beat on a high speed for two minutes until it is well combined and smooth. Alternatively, you could use an electric hand-held whisk.

4. Divide the mixture evenly between the prepared tins and bake in the preheated oven for 25–30 minutes until golden brown. The cake will look slightly darker than you might expect with the added malted milk powder, so be more vigilant in checking that it is ready.

5. To make the buttercream, heat the milk and malted milk powder in a small saucepan. Whisk until all the lumps of powder have dissolved and the mixture has thickened slightly. Set aside to cool. Beat the butter in a large bowl until smooth, then gradually add the icing sugar and cool malted milk paste. Use an electric hand-held whisk to beat the buttercream for 5–10 minutes until light and fluffy. It should hold its shape but still be fairly soft.

6. To assemble the cake, stack the bottom two layers on top of each other and use a circular 9cm cutter to remove the middle. Press through both layers at once to make sure the holes line up.

7. Put the bottom ring on a cake stand and cover the top with a layer of buttercream using a palette knife. Try not to get icing too close to the middle, because moisture on the sweets will cause them to become sticky.

8. Put the second ring on top of the first and fill the hole with milk bottle sweets. Make sure it is filled to the same level as the sponge or the top sponge will cave in. Cover the second ring with buttercream then add the final sponge. Thinly cover the whole cake with some of the buttercream to trap any crumbs, then chill for a minimum of 30 minutes.

9. Cover the cake with the remaining buttercream, placing a large dollop on the top to create a swirl. Decorate using more milk bottle sweets and coloured paper straws.

Tiramisu

CHOCOLATE TRUFFLE LOAF

· uses up ·
· leftover
· chocolates ·

BUNDT CAKE

×2

LOAF CAKE

· SPECTACULAR ·
DESSERT ·

FAVOURITE CHOCOLATE cake RECIPE

×1

DELICIOUS
CENTREPIECES

×2

×2

EVERYDAY ·
INDULGENCE ·

18cm LAYER CAKE

21cm SANDWICH CAKE

BLACKBERRY &
HONEYCOMB
OMBRE CAKE

MINT CHOCOLATE
ICE-CREAM CAKE

Chocolate and
passionfruit
layer cake

MY FAVOURITE CHOCOLATE CAKE

Chocolate cake absolutely has to be two things: dark and moist. A dry chocolate cake hits you in the back of the throat with its coarse crumbs, like a tickly cough. To make sure it is sticky and dense I use buttermilk. This might seem a curious ingredient to include in a chocolate cake, but it is completely necessary to guarantee a moist and tender crumb. Essentially sour milk (not the same thing as soured, spoiled milk!), its acidity reacts with the bicarbonate of soda to give this cake its rise. It also acts as a tenderiser, stopping tough gluten networks forming so quickly. If you can't find buttermilk, mix some milk with lemon juice as a substitute. The juice will make the milk curdle, but don't worry about this.

Adding coffee to chocolate cakes really brings out the flavour in the cocoa, and you can barely taste it. If you detest coffee or are baking for children, you can use boiling water instead in any of the chocolate cake recipes.

MAKES ONE 20cm SPONGE LAYER

Butter, for greasing
125g plain flour
225g caster sugar
50g cocoa powder
1 tsp bicarbonate of soda
¼ tsp salt
125ml buttermilk
    (cultured), or 110ml milk
    plus ½ tbsp lemon juice
60g butter, melted
1 egg
125ml coffee (or water)

You will also need a 20cm tin.

1. Preheat the oven to 180°C/160°C fan/gas 4 then grease a 20cm tin and line it with baking parchment. Put the plain flour, caster sugar, cocoa powder, bicarbonate of soda and salt into a large bowl. Whisk to combine.

2. If you don't have buttermilk, pour the milk into a large jug and add the lemon juice. Leave to stand for five minutes until thickened.

3. Whisk the buttermilk/acidified milk into the melted butter and egg followed by the coffee or water.

4. Pour the wet mixture into the dry ingredients, whisking until a smooth batter has formed. It will be very runny, and if you are making more than one layer, the best way to divide it between the tins is to transfer the batter to a large jug. You can then use either the markings on the jug to measure the amount going into each tin, or put a tin on the scales and measure by weight. It is important to do this so that the layers are the same height and cook at the same rate.

5. Bake for 25–30 minutes until risen and a skewer inserted comes out clean. Leave to cool in the tin for ten minutes before turning out onto a cooling rack.

CHOCOLATE AND PASSIONFRUIT LAYER CAKE

Chocolate cake is a beautiful thing on its own, but adding a thick layer of sharp passionfruit curd undercuts the heavy richness and balances the sweetness – which dangerously means that one slice is no longer enough...

SERVES 10

Butter, for greasing
2 x My Favourite Chocolate
    Cake recipe (page 59)

FILLING
150ml double cream
1 tbsp icing sugar
10 tbsp passionfruit curd,
    with or without seeds
    (page 21)

ICING
50g butter
100g dark chocolate,
    chopped
75g icing sugar
1 tsp milk
Sprinkle of chocolate
    shavings, to decorate

You will also need two 20cm
round tins.

1. Preheat the oven to 180°C/160°C fan/gas 4 then grease two 20cm tins and line with baking parchment.

2. Make two batches of My Favourite Chocolate Cake recipe and use it to fill the tins.

3. Bake for 25–30 minutes until risen and a skewer inserted comes out clean. Leave to cool in the tin for ten minutes before turning out onto a cooling rack.

4. Whip the cream and icing sugar together in a small bowl until it forms soft peaks and holds its shape when mixed. Be careful to stop when it reaches soft peaks or you might over-whip the cream, which will ruin the finished cake.

5. Spread the whipped cream all over the top of one of the sponges, then cover with spoonfuls of passionfruit curd. Carefully sandwich the second sponge on top.

6. To make the icing, melt the butter and chocolate together in a microwave or in a heatproof bowl over a pan of simmering water. Remove from the heat and mix in the icing sugar and the milk, then use a palette knife to spread it over the top of the cake. Sprinkle over chocolate shavings before serving. Keep any leftover cake in the fridge, where it will keep well for 2–3 days.

CHOCOLATE TRUFFLE LOAF

Another name for this simple chocolate loaf is a Chocolate Box Cake. It is a great way of making the last few leftover chocolates into something really delicious. You can use any flavour or type of chocolate you fancy – I'd really recommend it with my Amaretto Truffles or Peanut Butter Balls (see pages 212 and 215).

SERVES 8–10

Butter, for greasing
1 x My Favourite Chocolate
  Cake recipe (page 59)

ICING
75g butter
150g dark chocolate,
  chopped
100g icing sugar
1 tsp milk

TO DECORATE
5–6 chocolate truffles

You will also need a 1-litre loaf tin.

1. Preheat the oven to 180°C/160°C fan/gas 4 then grease a 1-litre loaf tin and line with baking parchment.

2. Make My Favourite Chocolate Cake recipe then pour into the loaf tin.

3. Bake for 40–45 minutes until risen and a skewer inserted comes out clean. Leave to cool in the tin until completely cold.

4. To make the icing, melt the butter and chocolate together in a heatproof bowl, either in the microwave or over a pan of simmering water. Remove from the heat, then sift over the icing sugar and beat until smooth. Stir in the milk and mix in thoroughly.

5. Spread the icing over the cooled loaf cake, then top with some chopped and some whole truffles. I use my Amaretto Truffles, but you could use any kind. This cake keeps really well at room temperature for up to one week.

TIRAMISU BUNDT CAKE

One of the first cakes I made when I started baking was a variation on this tiramisu cake, which used leftover chocolate cake to form the layers. As is traditional in tiramisu, the sponge was soaked with a strong coffee and sweet dessert wine mixture, which I was brushing liberally over the cake. It was certainly an interesting conversation starter for my parents and their dinner guests, after they found a 12-year-old brandishing a large bottle of dessert wine alone in the kitchen...

SERVES 8–10

Butter, for greasing
2 x My Favourite Chocolate
  Cake recipe (page 59)
125ml strong espresso

SOAKING SYRUP
50ml strong coffee
4 tbsp sweet dessert wine or
  Tia Maria

FILLING
250g mascarpone
500ml double cream
1 tbsp icing sugar
Cocoa powder, to dust

You will also need a curved 1.5-litre bundt or chiffon cake tin.

1. Preheat the oven to 170°C/150°C fan/gas 3, thoroughly grease a curved bundt or chiffon cake tin with butter then dust with flour. This will make it easier to turn the cake out once baked.

2. Make two batches of My Favourite Chocolate Cake recipe, adding espresso instead of weaker coffee in step 3.

3. Pour into the tin and bake for 45–50 minutes until risen and a skewer inserted comes out clean.

4. Leave to cool in the tin before removing and slicing into three even layers. Put the bottom layer onto a cake stand. Mix together the coffee and alcohol and liberally brush the cold sponge on the stand with a third of the syrup.

5. To make the filling, mix the mascarpone with the double cream and icing sugar and beat until smooth. Spoon half the filling into a disposable piping bag and cut the tip off to make a 2cm hole. Pipe small peaks all over the bottom sponge, then put the second layer on top.

6. Brush the next third of the soaking syrup over the second layer and repeat the piping process. Brush the remaining liquid over the bottom of the final layer before placing on top. Pipe a few peaks neatly around the top, then dust with cocoa powder. Store any uneaten cake in the fridge; it gets better with age so try it on the second or third day!

MINT CHOCOLATE ICE-CREAM CAKE

I made this cake for my little sister's fifteenth birthday party and it was a real hit. I love the dripping chocolate effect, it makes any cake look so appealing and it is really easy to achieve. Mint chocolate chip is my favourite ice-cream flavour, and the freshness of the mint works really well with the intensity of the chocolate.

SERVES 10–12

Butter, for greasing
2 x My Favourite Chocolate
   Cake recipe (page 59)

BUTTERCREAM
250g unsalted butter,
   softened
600g icing sugar
1 tsp peppermint extract
1–2 tsp milk
Green gel food colouring
25g dark chocolate,
   chopped into very small
   cubes

ICE-CREAM
100g dark chocolate,
   chopped
1 ice-cream cone
Sprinkles, to decorate

DRIZZLE
125g dark chocolate,
   chopped
75g butter

You will also need three
18cm round tins and an
electric hand-held whisk.

1. Preheat the oven to 180°C/160°C fan/gas 4 then grease three 18cm tins and line with baking parchment.

2. Make two batches of My Favourite Chocolate Cake recipe, divide between the tins then bake for 25–30 minutes until risen and a skewer inserted comes out clean. Leave to cool in the tin for ten minutes before turning out onto a cooling rack.

3. To make the buttercream, beat the butter and icing sugar together using an electric hand-held whisk until really light and fluffy. Start on a slow speed to mix in the sugar, then turn up the speed to incorporate as much air as possible. Add the peppermint extract and enough milk to loosen the icing a little. Add a tiny amount of green food colouring, being really careful to tint the icing just enough to resemble the classic ice-cream – you don't want it too dark.

4. Sift the dark chocolate cubes to remove any chocolate dust or flakes as these will turn the icing brown and make it look less authentic. Fold the chips into the icing by hand.

5. Use a palette knife to spread some of the mint buttercream onto each cake, then stack the layers on top of each other. Cover the whole cake with the remaining icing, smoothing the top and sides as much as possible. You don't need to crumb coat this cake, as the chocolate crumbs will blend into the mint chocolate chip icing. Chill the cake for at least 30 minutes.

6. To make the ice-cream ball, melt the chocolate in a small heatproof bowl over a pan of simmering water. When it is completely melted, add 1 tablespoon of water and stir quickly. The chocolate will seize and go grainy, which while usually undesirable, creates a great ball of 'ice-cream'. You may need to add a little more water. When the mixture is thick, use an ice-cream scoop to make a large ball. Gently put into the cone and leave to cool.

7. To make the chocolate drizzle, melt the chocolate and butter together in another small heatproof bowl over a pan of simmering water. When smooth, leave to cool for five minutes before carefully pouring over the top of the chilled cake. Use the back of a spoon to encourage the glaze to run over the edges of the cake.

8. Put the ice-cream cone face down into the middle of the glaze, then arrange a few sprinkles around the centre.

BLACKBERRY AND HONEYCOMB OMBRE CAKE

Ombre cakes are so elegant, and much simpler to create than people think. My buttercream gets its pinky hue from blackberry syrup rather than food colouring, so you get their delicate, autumnal flavour in every bite.

The honeycomb should be made and put on top of the cake just before serving, because when it is left out in the air it starts to weep and becomes sticky pools of sugar rather than glorious, bubbly shards. I make this cake in smaller 18cm tins to add extra height, so it only needs two batches of My Favourite Chocolate Cake recipe.

SERVES 10–12

Butter, for greasing
2 x My Favourite Chocolate
   Cake recipe (page 59)

JAM
150g blackberries
100g caster sugar

HONEYCOMB
100g caster sugar
4 tbsp golden syrup
1½ tsp bicarbonate of soda

BUTTERCREAM
250g unsalted butter,
   softened
600g icing sugar
1 tsp milk

TO DECORATE
12 blackberries
Mint leaves (optional)

You will also need three 18cm round tins and an electric hand-held whisk.

1. Preheat the oven to 180°C/160°C fan/gas 4 then grease three 18cm tins and line with baking parchment.

2. Make two batches of My Favourite Chocolate Cake recipe and divide between the three tins.

3. Bake for 25–30 minutes until risen and a skewer inserted comes out clean. Leave to cool in the tins for ten minutes before turning out onto a cooling rack.

4. To make the jam, put the blackberries, sugar and 50ml of water into a small saucepan and simmer for 15 minutes. Stir often, gently crushing the blackberries so they release their colour. Drain the purple syrup into a small heatproof jug using a sieve, and reserve the pulp to fill the cakes.

5. To make the honeycomb, put the sugar and golden syrup into a medium saucepan. Boil until it turns a dark golden colour, then remove from the heat and quickly whisk in the bicarbonate of soda. The mixture will froth up and is extremely hot, so be careful. Pour out onto a piece of baking parchment and leave to harden before breaking into shards.

6. To make the buttercream, beat the butter and icing sugar together until smooth and light. This takes around ten minutes with an electric hand-held whisk. Put one third of the icing into a small bowl and add five teaspoons of the blackberry syrup. Repeat with another third in a separate bowl, only using one teaspoon of syrup this time. If the icing splits, add a few tablespoons of icing sugar and it should come back together. Add the milk to the remaining white icing to loosen it slightly. You should now have three different shades of icing that are all the same consistency.

7. Take the cooled sponges and sandwich them together with a little of the white icing and the pulp leftover from making the syrup. Cover the top and sides of the top layer of the cake with the white icing, applying it thickly as a lot will be scraped off later.

8. Cover the bottom third of the cake with a thick layer of the darkest icing, then fill in the gap between the two colours with the pale purple. Use a large palette knife, set at a 45° angle to the cake, to scrape off the excess icing and create a smooth finish. The colours should blend together slightly, creating the ombre effect.

9. Transfer the leftover icing into a piping bag fitted with a closed star nozzle. You can gently mix all the colours together to get a rippled effect. Pipe a wiggly border around the top of the cake, then decorate with honeycomb, blackberries and a few mint leaves, if you like.

MY FAVOURITE GINGER CAKE

There are few things more comforting than a big slab of sticky, moist ginger cake with its warm and spicy flavour. You get the gorgeous stickiness in this cake by using the melting method. Melting the fat with the sugars before adding the flour starts off the caramelisation process, allowing the sugar to melt more quickly when it is baked. Some brownies and blondies use the same technique, which gives a lovely chewiness and crumbs that easily stick together when pressed between your fingers.

Try to bake this as soon as you add the bicarbonate of soda, because the acidic treacle and dark sugars react with it, creating carbon dioxide, which makes the cake rise. If you wait, a lot of the gas will escape and the cake won't rise as well.

MAKES ONE 18cm CAKE

100g butter, plus extra for greasing

125g dark muscovado sugar

50g treacle

50g golden syrup

1 ball stem ginger, from a jar in syrup

100ml whole milk

1 egg

125g plain flour

½ tsp bicarbonate of soda

½ tsp ground ginger

½ tsp ground cinnamon

You will also need an 18cm round tin.

1. Preheat the oven to 160°C/140°C fan/gas 3 then grease an 18cm tin and line with baking parchment.

2. Heat the butter, sugar, treacle and syrup together in a large saucepan, stirring until the butter is melted and the sugar has dissolved. Melting the fat and sugar together gives ginger cake its characteristic stickiness, so make sure the mixture is smooth and there are no grains of sugar visible. Finely chop the stem ginger.

3. Add the milk to the saucepan and whisk until combined. This will cool the mixture down before you add the egg, stopping it from scrambling. Beat in the egg then stir in the chopped stem ginger.

4. Sift the flour, bicarbonate of soda and spices together in a large bowl. Pour the wet mixture over the top and beat together until smooth.

5. Pour into the tin then bake in the middle of the preheated oven for 40–50 minutes, or until firm and a skewer inserted comes out clean. Leave to cool completely in the tin before removing and adding toppings or enjoying just as it is.

GINGER AND CANDIED LEMON CREAM CAKE

Lemon and cream seem deceptively simple additions to a ginger cake, but this is a dream to eat. The sharpness of the lemon and the warm, spicy notes in the sponge give the illusion of something far more complex – which makes it a firm favourite in my family.

SERVES 10

Butter, for greasing
2 x My Favourite Ginger
    Cake recipe (opposite)

FILLING
100g full-fat cream cheese
150ml double cream
4 tbsp ginger syrup, from
    the stem ginger jar
2 tbsp icing sugar
8 tbsp lemon curd (page 21)

CANDIED PEEL
1 unwaxed lemon
75g caster sugar
50g granulated sugar

You will also need two 18cm round tins.

1. Preheat the oven to 160°C/140°C fan/gas 3 then grease two 18cm tins and line with baking parchment.

2. Make two batches of My Favourite Ginger Cake recipe, divide the mixture between the cake tins and bake for 40–50 minutes or until firm and a skewer inserted comes out clean. Allow to cool before filling.

3. To make the filling, whip the cream cheese, double cream, syrup and icing sugar together until thick enough to hold its shape.

4. For the candied peel, remove the lemon zest with a vegetable peeler. Try to get as little of the white pith as possible, because it is bitter and unpleasant. Finely slice the zest into long strands, then put in a saucepan with the caster sugar and 50ml of water. Boil for ten minutes or until translucent, then drain, toss in granulated sugar and leave to dry out on a baking tray covered in baking parchment.

5. To assemble, put one of the cakes onto a plate or cake stand. Spread three-quarters of the cream cheese icing over the bottom layer, and top with the lemon curd. Sandwich the second layer on top, and decorate with the remaining icing and the candied peel. This cake will keep in the fridge for up to a week, and the sponge improves with age so it could be made 3–4 days in advance.

GINGER AND WHITE CHOCOLATE LOAF

White chocolate can sometimes be sickly sweet but mixing it with tangy crème fraîche gives it a lighter, fresher taste. You can make the crystallised ginger yourself by boiling pieces of fresh ginger in a sugar syrup until tender, then tossing them in granulated sugar.

SERVES 8–10

Butter, for greasing
1 x My Favourite Ginger
   Cake recipe (page 68)

ICING
50g white chocolate,
   chopped
100g crème fraîche
5 pieces of crystallised stem
   ginger, quartered

You will also need a 1kg loaf tin.

1. Preheat the oven to 160°C/140°C fan/gas 3 and grease and line a 1kg loaf tin. Leave an overhang of baking parchment so the cake is easy to lift out.

2. Make My Favourite Ginger Cake recipe, pour into the loaf tin and bake for 45–50 minutes or until a skewer inserted comes out clean. Leave to cool in the tin.

3. To make the icing, melt the white chocolate. (As white chocolate burns so easily, I find the best way to do this is to put the chocolate into a small plastic container with a lid and leave it to stand in boiling water.) The chocolate takes 5–7 minutes to melt fully.

4. Beat the crème fraîche in a small bowl and pour in the melted chocolate. Continue to beat until thickened, then spread all over the top of the cooled loaf. Arrange the chunks of ginger on the top before serving. If not serving immediately, store in the fridge for up to three days until you are ready to eat it.

GINGER AND RHUBARB CAKE

If I could get away with putting candied rhubarb twirls on every bake, I would. They are simple to make and have the most delicious sweet yet tangy flavour.

SERVES 8–10

Butter, for greasing
1 x My Favourite Ginger
    Cake recipe (page 68)

RHUBARB FILLING
200g rhubarb
100g caster sugar

CANDIED RHUBARB
100g rhubarb
Pink gel food colouring

RUNNY ICING
150g icing sugar

You will also need an 18cm round tin.

1. Preheat the oven to 160°C/140°C fan/gas 3. Grease an 18cm tin and line with baking parchment.

2. Chop the rhubarb for the filling into 5cm-long pieces and put into a saucepan with the caster sugar and 100ml of water. Bring to the boil and simmer for five minutes, or until the rhubarb is soft but not disintegrating. Remove the rhubarb with a slotted spoon and put on a sheet of kitchen paper to cool. Keep the cooking syrup for step 6.

3. Make My Favourite Ginger Cake recipe up to step 3. Pour the mixture into the prepared tin then arrange the chunks of rhubarb on top. They will sink into the middle of the cake, so don't worry about being tidy.

4. Bake for 35–40 minutes or until a skewer inserted comes out clean and the cake no longer wobbles. Allow the cake to cool completely in the tin. Meanwhile, turn the oven down to 120°C/100°C fan/gas ½.

5. To make the rhubarb twirls, trim the ends off the sticks of rhubarb and use a vegetable peeler to peel them into long thin strips. Put the peeler at the top and pull down firmly along the length, to get clean-cut pieces. Discard the first layer of peelings, as the skin will not dry out as well as the flesh.

6. Gently heat the syrup left over from the boiled rhubarb with a tiny amount of pink food colouring, and remove from the heat. Dip the rhubarb strips into the syrup one by one then put onto a parchment lined baking tray. Bake the strips for one hour (baking the fruit on a low temperature like this dries it out and makes it crisp).

7. Find a spoon handle or chopstick that is a perfect cylinder. Once the rhubarb strips are done, remove them from the oven and, working quickly as they will harden as they cool, take a warm strip and wrap it around the cylinder. It should harden quickly and slide off easily. If the rhubarb is still sticky or hardens too fast, return it to the oven to soften and dry a little more before trying again. Repeat with all the strips to create crisp, pink curls.

8. To make the icing, mix the icing sugar with 2–3 tablespoons of water, or until it is a thick but runny paste. Spread the icing over the cake, using a palette knife or the back of a spoon to encourage it to drip down the sides, then top with the rhubarb curls. This cake will keep for 4–5 days – if it lasts that long!

PISTACHIO AND LIME COURGETTE CAKE

It sounds peculiar, but I promise that you will love this cake. It is not just another food fad – courgette in a cake really does work! I was sceptical at first too, but upon trying a bite of the incredibly moist sponge with the zingy lime icing, you will not look at a courgette in the same way again.

SERVES 8–10

Butter, for greasing
250g courgettes, around
   2–3 small ones
2 eggs
125ml vegetable oil
150g caster sugar
225g self-raising flour
½ tsp baking powder
¼ tsp salt
Zest of ½ an unwaxed lime

ICING
100g full-fat cream cheese
250g icing sugar
Zest and juice of ½ an
   unwaxed lime
30g pistachio nuts

You will also need a 20cm round tin.

1. Preheat the oven to 180°C/160°C fan/gas 4 then grease a 20cm tin and line with baking parchment.

2. Grate the courgettes coarsely (there is no need to peel them); if they are grated too finely they will turn to mush.

3. Put the eggs, oil and sugar in a bowl then beat by hand until creamy. Fold in the flour, baking powder and salt. Stir in the courgette and the zest. The mixture does look unusual at this stage, but bear with it as it completely transforms when baked!

4. Pour the mixture into the prepared tin and bake for 35–40 minutes, until golden on top and firm to touch or a skewer inserted comes out clean. Remove from the oven and leave to cool completely in the tin before removing and decorating.

5. To make the icing, beat the cream cheese, icing sugar and lime juice together until smooth. Spread on the top of the cooled cake.

6. Chop the pistachio nuts and sprinkle them over the cake, then top with the remaining lime zest.

CARROT, BLUEBERRY AND ORANGE CAKE

Carrot cake is the king of all vegetable cakes, and I've added a few new flavours into this British classic. Cooking blueberries releases their aromatic flavour and adds bursts of colour through the sponge, and orange brings a real freshness. You could cover the sides of the cake too, but I think it is a welcome change being able to admire the tall layers.

SERVES 10–12

Butter, for greasing
300g soft light brown sugar
3 eggs
300ml sunflower oil
300g plain flour
1 tsp bicarbonate of soda
1 tsp baking powder
½ tsp salt
½ tsp ground cinnamon
1 tsp ground ginger
Zest and juice of 1 large
    unwaxed orange
250g carrots, grated
100g macadamia nuts,
    roughly chopped
100g blueberries
Blueberries and orange zest
    shavings, to decorate

ICING
500g mascarpone
200g icing sugar

You will also need three
18cm round tins.

1. Preheat the oven to 180°C/160°C fan/gas 4 then grease and line three 18cm tins.

2. In a large bowl, whisk together the sugar, eggs and oil until the mixture is smooth.

3. In a separate bowl, combine the flour, bicarbonate of soda, baking powder, salt and spices, before folding them into the wet mixture. Stir the dry ingredients in gently until no large floury pockets remain – you don't want to stir too many times or the resulting cake will be tough.

4. Add the orange zest, juice, grated carrots, nuts and blueberries and mix gently until all the ingredients are well combined. Divide evenly between the three tins, then bake for 30–35 minutes or until a skewer inserted comes out clean. Leave to cool for ten minutes in the tins before transferring to a cooling rack to cool completely.

5. To make the icing, beat the mascarpone with the icing sugar until smooth and spreadable. Spread the icing between each layer of cake, then top with blueberries and shavings of orange zest.

PUMPKIN SPICE CAKE

To complete my trio of vegetable cakes, I give you the pumpkin spice cake. You'll notice immediately that this is very different in texture, as the pumpkin is puréed rather than grated. Once mixed in, the dispersed purée locks moisture into every single crumb of this cake, giving it a velvety smoothness that few cakes can recreate. If you can't get hold of pumpkin purée, you can easily make your own by boiling chunks of pumpkin or squash until soft, then puréeing them in a food processor.

SERVES 10–12

Butter, for greasing
500g plain flour, plus extra
   for dusting
1 x 425g tin pumpkin purée
4 eggs
200ml vegetable oil
150ml whole milk
250g caster sugar
250g light brown sugar
2 tsp bicarbonate of soda
1 tsp salt
1¼ tsp ground cinnamon
½ tsp ground nutmeg
½ tsp ground ginger
⅛ tsp ground cloves

TOPPING
200g icing sugar
Ground cinnamon and
   nutmeg, to dust

You will also need a 1.5-litre bundt tin.

1. Preheat the oven to 180°C/160°C fan/gas 4 and grease and lightly flour a 1.5-litre bundt tin. As this cake has a high sugar content, it is more likely to caramelise and stick to the tin, so the layer of flour helps prevent this.

2. In a large mixing bowl, beat together the pumpkin purée, eggs, oil, milk and both sugars until they are well blended.

3. Using another bowl, combine the flour, bicarbonate of soda, salt and spices. Fold the dry ingredients into the wet ingredients and mix until smooth, with no large lumps of flour remaining.

4. Pour into the prepared tin and bake for 50 minutes, or until a skewer inserted comes out clean. Leave the cake to cool for 10–15 minutes, or until the pan is cool enough to touch. Use a plastic spatula or knife and run it around the edges of the tin if the cake looks like it might be stuck. Invert onto a cooling rack and leave to cool completely before decorating.

5. For the topping, mix the icing sugar with 1 tablespoon of water to make a thick paste. Transfer to a piping bag, cut a medium-sized hole in the tip and pipe a thick ring around the top of the cold bundt, then tap the cooling rack firmly on the work surface to encourage the icing to start spreading and to drip down the edges. Dust with a little nutmeg and cinnamon before moving the cake to a cake stand or large plate to serve. This cake will stay beautifully moist for 5–6 days.

BISCUITS

EVOLUTION OF THE

MACARON

ROSE
LAVENDER · mint
Delicate

PEACH
Bellini
COSMOPOLITAN · MOJITO
ALCOHOLIC

CHOCOLATE · Lemon
vanilla · COFFEE
CLASSIC

PASSIONFRUIT
GINGERBREAD · PEANUT BUTTER Jelly
UNUSUAL

PISTACHIO · Almond · HAZELNUT · PEANUT
GROUND NUTS

MACARONS

You can make macarons using French or Italian meringue as the base, but I would suggest Italian.

In a French meringue, sugar is added to the eggs while whisking them, whereas, in Italian meringue, hot sugar syrup is added instead. Although a little trickier to make, cooking the egg whites with the syrup creates a more stable foam. It is less temperamental than French meringue and more forgiving during the mixing process, which will stop the macarons spreading too much.

Italian meringue is easiest to make if you have a stand mixer, but if you don't you can still use an electric hand-held whisk; just be extra careful with the hot sugar.

There are two ways to get perfectly round macarons – one is to draw around something roughly 4cm in diameter on the back of a piece of baking parchment with a pencil, and the other is to print off a template of 4cm circles that you can slip under the parchment. I find the latter easier, and you can reuse the template later.

MY FAVOURITE MACARONS

MAKES 35

160g ground almonds
180g icing sugar
120g egg white (from about 3 large eggs)
160g caster sugar
gel food colouring (optional)

You will also need a food processor, stand mixer or electric hand-held whisk and a sugar thermometer.

1. Put two 4cm circle templates (see page 81) on two baking trays then cover each with a layer of baking parchment. (Or draw around something roughly 4cm in diameter directly onto the baking parchment.)

2. Place the ground almonds and icing sugar into the bowl of a food processor. Blitz until the nuts are really finely ground and well mixed into the sugar. I used to skip this step, thinking it unnecessary, but it is the key to smooth, even macarons. Coarse bits of almond in the batter weigh it down, making it grainy. Transfer the mixture into a large bowl.

3. Mix half the egg white (60g) into the finely ground almonds and icing sugar and stir until a stiff paste forms. Set this aside while you make the Italian meringue.

4. Place the caster sugar into a small saucepan with 3 tablespoons of water. Bring to the boil and stir until the sugar has dissolved. When the mixture is clear, stop stirring and heat until the syrup registers 118°C on a sugar thermometer. Meanwhile, put the remaining egg white into a clean, grease-free bowl (any droplets of fat can deflate meringue). As the syrup is nearing 118°C, start whisking the egg white on a high speed in a stand mixer or with an electric hand-held whisk until it reaches soft peaks and just holds its shape on the whisk.

5. Take the syrup off the heat as soon as it is up to temperature and, with the whisk on low, slowly pour the syrup into the egg whites in a steady stream. Make sure you don't stop whisking, and try to avoid pouring the syrup onto the beaters or it will get messy. Continue to whisk on a high speed until the mixture has cooled slightly and the bowl is no longer hot to touch. It should be thick and glossy. Add any gel food colouring now, if using, as it is easiest to mix it through the macaron mixture at this stage.

6. Use a spatula to scrape the meringue out of the bowl and onto the almond paste in the large bowl. Fold together until the mixture runs in a thick ribbon from the spatula, disappearing back into the mix within ten seconds. If the mixture is too thick, the piping bag will leave peaks and the shells will not be smooth. Transfer to a piping bag fitted with a 1cm-round nozzle. Pipe 4cm circles onto the baking parchment, using the templates (or drawn circles) as a guide.

7. Leave the macarons to dry for at least 30 minutes until a thin skin forms on top; it may take a little longer if the kitchen is humid. They should no longer be sticky to the touch and will have a matt appearance. The

skin allows the macarons to withstand the oven temperature for long enough to rise and let the signature 'foot' (the lacy bit at the bottom of a macaron) peek out. While you are waiting, preheat the oven to 170°C/150°C fan/gas 2.

8. Bake in the centre of the oven, one tray at a time, for ten minutes. The shells should not have started to brown, but they should be firm and sound hollow when lightly tapped. Leave to cool for a few minutes before peeling off the parchment.

PEACH BELLINI MACARONS

These cocktail macarons (and those on pages 86–88) always take people by surprise! Colourful and fun with a contrasting sharp filling that balances the sweetness, they look great stacked in fluted or cocktail glasses, and would be fantastic served as a dessert or canapé for a party.

MAKES 35

1 x batch of macaron shells
(pages 82–83), coloured
orange

PURÉE
2 small ripe peaches
3 tbsp caster sugar
1 tsp lemon juice

BUTTERCREAM
50g unsalted butter,
softened
150g icing sugar
2 tbsp white wine or
prosecco

You will also need an electric hand-held whisk.

1. First, make the purée. Bring a small pan of water, big enough to fit the peaches in comfortably, to the boil. Mark a cross on the bottom of each peach using a sharp knife. Fill a separate bowl with ice-cold water.

2. When the water is boiling, drop the peaches into the pan. Allow to cook for 1–2 minutes, or until the skin starts to peel away. Carefully remove the peaches and fully submerge them in the cold water. This process makes the peaches easier to peel.

3. Remove the skins with your fingers and discard them, then slice the flesh into small pieces and discard the stones as well. Place the chunks into a food processor and blend until smooth, or press the mixture through a sieve.

4. Pour the peach purée into a small saucepan and add the sugar and lemon juice. Allow to gently simmer for 5–10 minutes, or until the mixture has thickened slightly and is no longer watery. Reducing the purée like this helps to prevent the macaron shells going soggy when they are assembled. Put into a small container and refrigerate until needed.

5. Next, make the buttercream. Put the softened butter and icing sugar into a large bowl and beat using an electric hand-held whisk until it forms a thick paste.

6. Add the white wine or prosecco to the buttercream, a tablespoon at a time, and whisk to combine. Continue whisking for a further five minutes to lighten the mixture; it should be pale and fluffy. If it splits, add a few tablespoons of icing sugar and it should come back together. Transfer to a piping bag and refrigerate until needed.

7. To assemble the macarons, arrange the shells in pairs, discarding any misshapen or cracked shells (or keep them for my Macaron Shell Ice-cream on page 89!). Pipe a ring of buttercream onto half of the shells, then fill the centre of each ring with a teaspoonful of peach purée. Sandwich together with the other macaron shells. Store them on their sides (to stop the filling seeping through the bottoms) for up to four days in the fridge.

COSMOPOLITAN MACARONS

The flavours in a Cosmopolitan are punchy – tart cranberry jelly is surrounded by a zingy Cointreau and vodka buttercream. If you want to make a non-alchoholic version, remove the alcohol and stir the zest of one orange into the buttercream.

MAKES 35

1 x batch of macaron shells
(pages 82–83), coloured
dark pink

CRANBERRY FILLING
150g frozen cranberries
4 tbsp caster sugar
1 tbsp vodka
2 tbsp Cointreau

BUTTERCREAM
50g unsalted butter,
softened
150g icing sugar
2 tbsp vodka
2 tbsp Cointreau

You will also need an electric hand-held whisk.

1. To make the filling, put the frozen cranberries into a small saucepan with the sugar, vodka and one tablespoon of the Cointreau. Simmer over a medium heat for 15 minutes, by which time the cranberries should have turned into a sticky pulp. If necessary, gently crush the berries with the back of the spatula to encourage them to burst.

2. Remove from the heat and stir in the remainder of the Cointreau. Push the mixture through a sieve into a small bowl; it will be quite difficult to push through. Don't forget to scrape the underside of the sieve as this is where most of the smooth filling gathers. Set this aside while you make the buttercream.

3. To make the buttercream, put the softened butter and icing sugar into a large bowl and beat using an electric hand-held whisk until it forms a thick paste.

4. Add the vodka and Cointreau to the mixture, a tablespoon at a time, and whisk to combine. Continue whisking the buttercream for a further five minutes to lighten it; it should be pale and fluffy. If the mixture looks like it has split, add a few tablespoons of icing sugar and it should come back together. Transfer to a piping bag and refrigerate until needed.

5. When ready to assemble the macarons, arrange the shells in pairs; discarding any misshapen or cracked shells (or keep them for my Macaron Shell Ice-cream on page 89!). Pipe a ring of buttercream onto half of the shells, then fill the centre of each ring with a teaspoonful of cranberry filling. Sandwich with the second macaron shell, repeat with the rest of the shells and mixture, and store them on their sides for up to four days in the fridge.

MOJITO MACARONS

This is one of my favourite cocktails in a fun, macaron size! I love the combination of fresh mint and lime curd – you can make your own curd by following the recipe on page 21.

MAKES 35

1 x batch of macaron shells (pages 82–83), coloured green

LIME AND MINT FILLING
4 tbsp lime curd (page 21)
Sprig of fresh mint or peppermint extract

BUTTERCREAM
50g unsalted butter, softened
150g icing sugar
4 tbsp white rum

SUGAR RIM
Zest of 1 unwaxed lime
75g caster sugar

You will also need an electric hand-held whisk.

1. Put the lime curd into a small bowl and stir briefly to loosen.

2. Finely chop the mint leaves, then stir them into the curd and mix until well combined. You will end up with a green, speckled curd. One or two drops of peppermint extract will also work, but this will give a much stronger flavour so take care when adding it to the curd. Set aside until needed.

3. To make the buttercream, put the softened butter and icing sugar into a large bowl and beat using an electric hand-held whisk until it forms a thick paste.

4. Add the white rum to the mixture, a tablespoon at a time, and whisk to combine. Continue whisking for a further five minutes to lighten the buttercream; it should be pale and fluffy. If the mixture looks like it has split, add a few tablespoons of icing sugar and it should come back together. Transfer the icing to a piping bag and refrigerate until needed.

5. Combine the lime zest and caster sugar in a small bowl.

6. Arrange the shells in pairs, discarding any misshapen or cracked shells (use them for my Macaron Shell Ice-cream, opposite). Pipe a ring of buttercream onto half of the shells, then fill the gap in the centre of each with a teaspoonful of lime and mint curd. Sandwich together with the other macaron shells then gently roll in the lime and sugar to give it a crunchy edge. Store them on their sides in the fridge to prevent the filling seeping through for up to four days.

MACARON SHELL ICE-CREAM

Before you master macarons, you will inevitably have a few flop batches that don't quite make the grade. While they might look like nothing special, even failed macarons have a wonderful nutty flavour and lovely texture, which shouldn't be wasted. This is my favourite recipe for using up leftover shells – a rich and creamy ice-cream studded with chewy almond pockets. Try adding whole berries to the mixture as it sets, for bursts of fresh flavour.

If you have an ice-cream maker, pour the mix into the machine at step 3. My recipe is churned by hand.

MAKES AROUND
1 LITRE OF
ICE-CREAM

2 large eggs
150g caster sugar
500ml double cream
250ml whole milk
1 tsp vanilla bean paste
150g macaron shells

You will also need an electric hand-held whisk.

1. Whisk the eggs and sugar together in a large mixing bowl with an electric hand-held whisk until they are light and fluffy; this will take 2–3 minutes.

2. Pour in the cream and milk, then gently mix in the vanilla bean paste. When the mixture is well combined, put the bowl into the freezer for 1½ hours, or until the ice-cream is just beginning to freeze around the edges.

3. Take the bowl out of the freezer and beat well, then return to the freezer for another hour before repeating the beating process twice more.

4. Fold in the macaron shells, then transfer the mixture to a large container. Freeze until solid before scooping and serving as a delicious dessert. No one will know it has come from an error! The ice-cream will keep for up to one month in the freezer.

COOKIES

For the last few years, I have been on a quest to find the best cookie recipe.

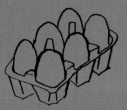

You know the kind: cookies that are buttery and crisp around the edges with a soft, chewy centre, cookies that have that cracked top, concealing butterscotch flavours and chunks of melted chocolate. Hundreds of cookies later, I am proud to present my favourite.

The type of sugar you use in a cookie dramatically changes both its flavour and texture. Brown sugar has a high moisture content and contains more molasses than white sugar, which provides chewiness and a stronger caramel flavour; however, it spreads less. Caster sugar, on the other hand, makes the cookie spread out more and gives it crunchy, crispy edges. A balance between the two is required to get cookies that are chewy and crispy, so don't compromise on either one. You could also use dark brown sugar instead of light brown for a stronger, treacly flavour. Some cookie recipes only use ordinary plain flour, which will deliver perfectly fine cookies, but I prefer to use a blend of strong plain and ordinary plain flour. Strong plain flour contains more gluten, which when mixed with wet ingredients like egg makes the cookie chewier.

Resting the cookie dough is the most tortuous part of the cookie-making process. But there's a good reason to do it! When you rest the dough, the flour proteins and starches can relax and respond to their environment, the flour can absorb the liquid more fully and the fat can solidify, allowing the dough to firm up, producing a better texture. The butterscotch flavour of the brown sugar is undeniably stronger in cookies that have been left to rest overnight or, better still, for two whole days.

The single biggest mistake that people make when baking cookies is over-baking them. As soon as they start to brown around the edges, get them out of the oven and then, a crucial and often neglected step, you need to leave them to cool down. They will not look like cookies yet, and will be very soft and puffy in the middle, but as you wait the hot sugars harden and the middle will firm up, making the cookies deliciously chewy.

MY FAVOURITE COOKIES

**MAKES 30 SMALL
OR 12 LARGE**

140g butter, softened, plus
    extra for greasing
120g light brown sugar
100g caster sugar
1 tsp vanilla extract
1 large egg
150g plain flour
100g strong plain flour
½ tsp bicarbonate of soda
½ tsp baking powder

1. In a large bowl, beat together the butter with both the sugars using a wooden spoon. Beat the mixture until well combined, but there is no need for it to be light and fluffy.

2. Add the vanilla extract and egg to the butter mixture and beat again until all the ingredients are smooth.

3. In a separate bowl, combine the remaining dry ingredients. You need the raising agents to be evenly distributed throughout the cookie dough so they all rise in the same way, so make sure they are well mixed.

4. Tip the dry ingredients into the wet mixture and fold in, using a spatula, until a stiff dough forms. Add any other ingredients, like chocolate chips or dried fruit, at this stage.

5. Refrigerate the dough for at least 30 minutes (up to 72 hours for optimum flavour and texture). Preheat the oven to 190°C/170°C fan/ gas 5. Grease two large baking trays and line with baking parchment.

6. Use a small or large ice-cream scoop (a teaspoon or tablespoon will work too, but the cookies won't be as regularly-shaped) to form balls of dough and place onto the trays, leaving enough space for each one to spread out. Try not to handle them too much, as the ragged top created by the scoop will give the cookies a traditional cracked surface.

7. Bake small cookies for ten minutes and large cookies for 15 minutes, or until the mixture has spread out and browned around the edges. Remove from the oven when they still look undercooked in the middle and allow to cool on the trays for at least ten minutes. These are best eaten freshly made and warm, but will keep for up to four days in a tin. I doubt they'll last that long!

SEA SALTED CARAMEL AND OAT COOKIES

Adding oats to these cookies gives them a chewy texture and works really well with the sticky caramel.

MAKES 30 SMALL OR 12 LARGE

1 x My Favourite Cookies recipe (opposite)
75g rolled oats
100g hard toffee
Pinch of sea salt

1. Make My Favourite Cookies recipe and add the oats to the flour mixture in step 3.

2. Chop the toffee into small pieces and mix into the dough in step 4. Refrigerate the dough for at least 30 minutes and bake as opposite.

3. When the biscuits come out of the oven, the toffee may have caused them to spread in different directions. Use a knife to push any edges back to form the circle again while the cookies are still warm. Finish with a sprinkle of sea salt.

CHAI AND MILK CHOCOLATE

Using chai powder is a great way of injecting a gentle yet unusual spice into a chocolate chip cookie. If you can't get hold of chai powder, try adding ½ teaspoon of ground cardamom, ¼ teaspoon of ground ginger and ¼ teaspoon of ground cloves for a similar flavour.

MAKES 30 SMALL OR 12 LARGE

1 x My Favourite Cookies recipe (opposite)
2 tbsp chai drink powder
1 tsp ground cinnamon
100g milk chocolate, chopped into small cubes

1. Make My Favourite Cookies recipe and add the chai powder and cinnamon to the flour mixture in step 3.

2. Add the chocolate to the dough in step 4. Refrigerate the dough for at least 30 minutes and bake as opposite.

NUT BUTTERS

It seems like a slightly magical thing to me that you can take a handful of dry, understated nuts and, with the help of a food processor, transform them into a luxurious, smooth butter.

Peanut butter is the most well known and you can use all nut butters in the same ways – on toast, as dips, squashed into dates or mixed into porridge – to inject a delicate nutty flavour.

Nut butter can be made from most nuts, and whether you roast them or not is up to you. Roasting deepens the flavour of nuts like peanuts and hazelnuts, and it can help get rid of any bitterness, for example in pecans. Some nuts, like cashews or macadamias, are great to use raw. You can choose to leave the skin on or off.

To make nut butters from scratch, you will need a powerful food processor as they require blending for quite a long time before the nuts release their natural oils and turn into a smooth paste. If you don't have one then I recommend either buying nut butters from health food shops, or finely chopping nuts and replacing some of the flour in a recipe with them, so you still get the flavour.

You'll never reach for a shop-bought jar of peanut butter again after you see how easy it is to make your own. You can flavour it with spices, syrup, honey or even cocoa powder to create a truly delicious spread. Plain nuts and a pinch of sea salt is all you need, so get blending.

MY FAVOURITE NUT BUTTER

**MAKES
1 LARGE JAR**

500g unseasoned whole
    nuts of your choice
Pinch of sea salt

You will also need a food
processor and a sterilised jar
(see page 19).

1. If you are roasting your nuts, preheat the oven to 180°C/160°C fan/ gas 4. Spread the nuts in one layer on a large baking tray and roast for 8–10 minutes, or until they begin to darken and smell more fragrant. It is important not to roast them for too long, or they will develop a bitter flavour, so remove from the oven as soon as they start to colour. Leave to cool completely before blending.

2. Tip the nuts into the food processor and pulse until they are coarsely ground. If you want crunchy butter, remove a quarter of the nuts at this stage and set aside to stir in later.

3. Blitz on full speed for 8–10 minutes, stopping every once in a while to scrape the sides down with a spatula. The paste will look dry and finely ground for a while, but be patient and the oils will eventually be teased out. If, after ten minutes, it still looks dry, you can add a few drops of vegetable oil to speed things up. Nuts with a high fat content, like macadamias and pecans, will blend quicker than lower-fat nuts like cashews. Make sure you wait for the mixture to be shiny and smooth; it will be runnier than the peanut butter you might buy at the shops.

4. Pour into a sterilised jar, or use straight away on toast or in one of my cookie recipes. The nut butter will keep for a few months in the fridge.

TWIST: CASHEW AND COCONUT BUTTER

Take 450g raw cashews and 50g desiccated coconut and put them into a food processor. Blitz until a smooth butter forms. Cashews have a higher carbohydrate and slightly lower fat content than other nuts like peanuts, so this might take a little longer. Add a few drops of vegetable oil if you are struggling to get a butter after ten minutes.

TWIST: MAPLE AND PECAN BUTTER

Roast 500g pecans as above then whizz in a food processor until a smooth butter forms. Drizzle in 50ml maple syrup and blend again. Pour into a sterilised jar, or stir it straight into a bowl of porridge!

MY FAVOURITE NUT COOKIES

Just when you thought cookies couldn't get any better, cookies enriched with nut butters come along. The extra fat found in nuts gives the cookies a delicious, melt-in-the-mouth texture and the delicate nutty flavours take biscuits to another level.

Nut butters contain both fats and starches, so they don't alter the consistency of your cookies too much. However, as different nuts have different fat contents, they can affect how the cookies spread. Pecan, peanut and macadamia butter cookies should be fine, but cookies made with cashew butter will not spread as much as you expect, since cashews contain more starch and less fat. This can be easily fixed, without sacrificing flavour, by gently pressing the cookies down with a palette knife or back of a spatula when they come out of the oven.

These cookies are a little thicker than their nut-free counterparts, but that is what makes them all the more indulgent.

MAKES 35 SMALL OR
15 LARGE

140g butter, softened, plus
    extra for greasing
120g light brown sugar
100g caster sugar
125g nut butter, crunchy
    or smooth (see opposite
    for ideas)
1 large egg, beaten
150g plain flour
100g strong plain flour
½ tsp bicarbonate of soda
½ tsp baking powder

1   Preheat the oven to 190°C/170°C fan/gas 5. Grease two large baking trays and line with baking parchment.

2. In a large bowl, beat together the butter with both the sugars using a wooden spoon. Beat the mixture until well combined, but there is no need for it to be light and fluffy. Stir in the nut butter and the beaten egg.

3. In a separate bowl, combine the remaining dry ingredients. You need the raising agents to be evenly distributed throughout the cookie dough so they all rise in the same way, so make sure they are well mixed.

4. Tip the dry ingredients into the wet mixture and fold in, using a spatula, until a stiff dough forms. Refrigerate the dough for at least 30 minutes (up to 72 hours for optimum flavour and texture).

5. Use a small or large ice-cream scoop (a teaspoon or tablespoon will work too, but the cookies won't be as regularly-shaped) to form balls of dough and place onto the baking trays, leaving enough space for each one to spread out. Try not to handle the dough too much, as the ragged top created by the scoop gives the cookies a traditional cracked surface.

6. Bake small cookies for ten minutes and large cookies for 15 minutes, or until the mixture has spread out and browned around the edges. Remove from the oven – they should look undercooked in the middle but they will firm up – and allow to cool for at least ten minutes before moving to a cooling rack.

TWIST: DATE, MAPLE AND PECAN COOKIES

Use 125g maple and pecan butter (page 96) as your nut butter, and add 150g chopped Medjool dates (6–7 dates) to the dough before you bake it. I love these with a steaming mug of coffee; the dates work really well with it.

TWIST: CASHEW, COCONUT AND MANGO COOKIES

Use 125g cashew and coconut butter (page 96) as your nut butter, and add 50g chopped white chocolate and 100g chopped dried mango to the dough before you bake it. Flatten them slightly before you put them into the oven.

TWIST: PEANUT BUTTER AND CHOCOLATE COOKIES

Use 125g crunchy peanut butter as your nut butter, and add 100g chopped dark chocolate and 50g chopped salted peanuts to the dough before you bake it. These are my personal favourite nut cookies – see if you agree!

CHOCOLATE AND LIME FLORENTINES

Florentines have a reputation for being difficult to make, but they are one of the quickest biscuits you can make and, providing you follow the recipe closely, they are very achievable. You can switch the dried fruits and nuts for whatever you like, but I love the combination of zingy lime with dark chocolate and sharp cranberries.

MAKES 20

50g plain flour

50g mixed peel, chopped

25g dried cranberries, thinly sliced

75g flaked almonds

Zest and juice of ½ an unwaxed lime

50g butter

50g light brown sugar

50g golden syrup

200g dark chocolate, chopped

1. Preheat the oven to 180°C/160°C fan/gas 4 and line a baking sheet with baking parchment.

2. In a small bowl, combine the flour, mixed peel and dried cranberries. Chop the almonds roughly and add them to the bowl with most of the lime zest.

3. Measure the lime juice, butter, sugar and syrup into a saucepan and heat on low until the butter has melted and the mixture is bubbling. Remove from the heat and allow to cool for a minute or two.

4. Tip the dry mixture into the caramel and stir until well combined. Use a teaspoon to spoon small amounts of mixture onto the prepared baking sheet, allowing lots of space for them to spread in the oven. You will need to cook two or three batches to use up the mixture.

5. Bake for 10–12 minutes, or until golden brown. If any of the florentines do not flatten out properly, use the back of a spatula to press them down. Remove from the oven and leave to harden before transferring to a cooling rack and repeating the process with the remaining mixture.

6. Melt the chocolate in a heatproof bowl over a pan of simmering water until the lumps have disappeared. If you want perfectly shiny chocolate, you could temper it (see how to do this on page 208), but it's not necessary. Use a palette knife or the back of a spoon to spread chocolate over the cooled florentines, then drag a fork through the chocolate to make wiggly lines. Sprinkle over the remaining lime zest and leave to cool.

TWIST: LEMON AND WHITE CHOCOLATE FLORENTINES

Swap the lime for lemon, the cranberries for 25g dried blueberries and the dark chocolate for 200g white chocolate.

BARS AND BROWNIES

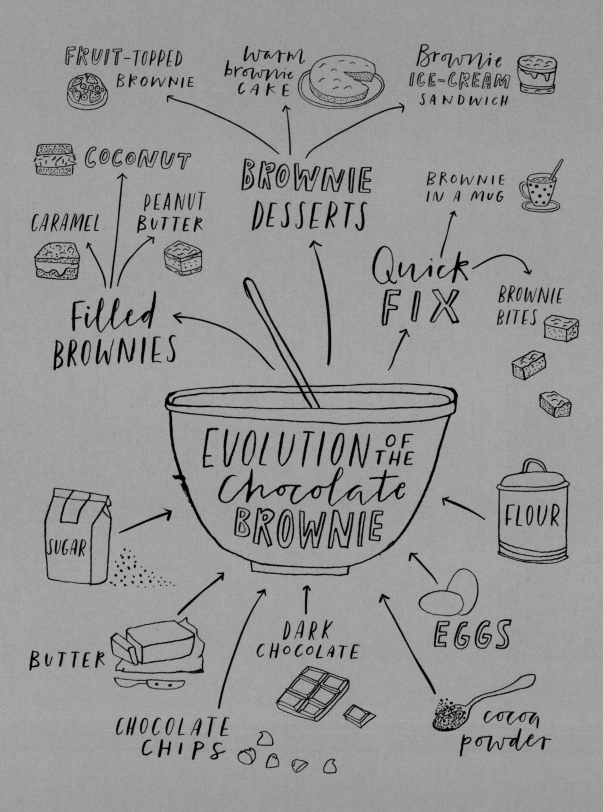

FRUIT-TOPPED BROWNIE

Warm brownie CAKE

Brownie ICE-CREAM SANDWICH

COCONUT

PEANUT BUTTER

CARAMEL

BROWNIE DESSERTS

BROWNIE IN A MUG

Quick FIX

BROWNIE BITES

Filled BROWNIES

EVOLUTION OF THE Chocolate BROWNIE

FLOUR

SUGAR

BUTTER

CHOCOLATE CHIPS

DARK CHOCOLATE

EGGS

cocoa powder

BROWNIES

People tend to be in one of two camps when it comes to brownies: those who like cakey, lighter brownies, and those who like dense, fudgy brownies.

I am very much in the second camp, a firm believer that brownies should be chewy, rich and indulgent. They should have enough substance that they hold together and are almost toffee-like to chew, and a velvety texture with little pockets of chocolate rippled all the way through.

At first glance, it may seem simple to achieve – if you want a lighter brownie, beat air in by mixing well, and if you want the dense kind, stir as little as possible. But there are other elements to consider.

First, to get the background butterscotch flavour and optimum chewiness, soft brown sugar is a great choice. It contains molasses, which makes it stickier than regular caster sugar and therefore ideal for chewy brownies. But too much molasses flavour can overwhelm the chocolate, so I use a mix of caster and soft brown sugar to complement the chocolate. It is important to start caramelising the sugar before mixing in the other ingredients to give these brownies their great texture.

Second, some brownie recipes use just cocoa powder, not chocolate as well, which makes a brownie with a wonderful texture but it is often not quite chocolatey enough. Using chocolate without any cocoa does give the desired flavour, but the added fat means that less gluten can develop, so the brownies don't hold together as effectively. So I use a mixture of chocolate and cocoa powder, which, as well as giving the best flavour, also makes the brownies lovely and chewy.

MY FAVOURITE BROWNIE

**MAKES ABOUT
24 SQUARES**

150g light brown sugar
225g caster sugar
225g butter
150g dark chocolate,
    chopped
3 eggs
115g plain flour
75g cocoa powder
150g chocolate chips

You will also need a
20 x 30cm brownie tin.

1. Preheat the oven to 200°C/180°C fan/gas 6 and line a 20 x 30cm tin with baking parchment.

2. Put the sugars and butter into a large saucepan and heat on medium until the butter has melted. Simmer the mixture for five minutes to allow the sugar to begin to melt, stirring all the time. It should lose its grainy appearance and the butter will combine with the sugar. Remove from the heat.

3. Add the chopped dark chocolate to the warm sugar and butter mixture and stir it in until it is completely melted. Leave to cool to room temperature.

4. When the mixture is cool enough to touch comfortably, beat in the eggs. Add the flour and cocoa powder before stirring briefly to combine. You don't want to overbeat the mixture or your brownies will become too 'cakey'. Fold through the chocolate chips and scrape into the prepared tin.

5. Bake for 20–25 minutes or until the top is shiny and slightly cracked. It will feel slightly underbaked, but for gooey, sticky brownies this is perfect. Leave to cool completely in the tin, then chill in the fridge for an hour to get the ultimate, fudgy centre, then cut into squares.

CHOCOLATE AND COCONUT BROWNIE

This brownie will surprise and win over any coconut-haters out there, or it has done in my experience. Two layers of rich chocolate brownie concealing a coconut-ice style layer of sticky coconut filling – it is coconut at its finest.

MAKES ABOUT
24 SMALL SQUARES
OR 12 LARGER BARS

1 x My Favourite Brownie
recipe (opposite)

FILLING
175g desiccated coconut
1 x 397g tin condensed milk
50g icing sugar

TO DECORATE
25g desiccated coconut

You will also need a
20 x 30cm brownie tin.

1. Line a 20 x 30cm tin with baking parchment.

2. Mix the coconut, condensed milk and icing sugar together in a small bowl until a thick paste forms. Press the mixture into the tin, trying to get it as flat as possible, then put into the freezer for at least one hour or until firm.

3. While the coconut filling is chilling, preheat the oven to 180°C/ 160°C fan/gas 4 and make My Favourite Brownie recipe up to step 4 but don't put the mixture in the tin yet.

4. Take the coconut and parchment out of the brownie tin then re-line the tin. Spoon half of the brownie mixture into the tin and spread thinly, so it covers the bottom completely. Press the coconut layer on top of the brownie – it should fit perfectly on top – peel the parchment off, then cover with the remaining brownie mixture.

5. Sprinkle the top of the brownie with coconut, then bake in the preheated oven for 20 minutes. The top should be shiny and slightly cracked, and the coconut on top lightly toasted.

6. Leave to cool completely before enjoying. Chilling the brownie in the fridge for three hours before eating will help it to firm up, giving it a soft and fudgy texture. Cut into squares or bars.

SALTED CARAMEL AND PRETZEL BROWNIE

Sweet and salty combinations have taken the world by storm, and this great recipe shows why. The salty pretzels on the top add a delicious crunch, but the recipe would work without them, too. Creating a slab of caramel that can be frozen means you will get an even layer of caramel in every bite and it is really easy to do.

MAKES ABOUT
14 BARS OR 45
BITE-SIZED PIECES

1 x My Favourite Brownie
recipe (page 106)

CARAMEL FILLING
200g caster sugar
75g butter
3 tbsp double cream
Pinch of sea salt

TO DECORATE
100g small pretzels

You will also need a
20 x 30cm brownie tin.

1. Line a 20 x 30cm tray with baking parchment.

2. To make the caramel filling, put the sugar and butter into a large, heavy-based saucepan with 50ml of water. Heat the mixture on a moderate heat, stirring all the time to stop the caramel sticking to the bottom of the saucepan. After about ten minutes, when the mixture is a dark golden caramel colour, remove from the heat and stir in the double cream and sea salt. Make sure you are using a long wooden spoon for this, as it will splutter quite violently. Pour into the tin and put into the freezer for at least 30 minutes to chill until completely solid.

3. While the caramel is chilling, preheat the oven to 200°C/180°C fan/ gas 6 and make My Favourite Brownie recipe up to step 4, but don't put the mixture in the tin yet.

4. Lift the caramel slab out of the baking tin and set aside. Spoon half of the brownie mixture into the same tin and spread thinly, so it covers the bottom completely. Press the set caramel layer on top of the brownie – it should fit perfectly on top – then cover with the remaining brownie mixture.

5. Arrange the pretzels in lines on the top, so they cover the whole surface, then bake in the preheated oven for 20 minutes. The top should be shiny and slightly cracked, and the caramel will start bubbling up around the edges.

6. Leave to cool completely before eating, because the caramel filling will be extremely hot.

BROWNIE ICE-CREAM SANDWICH

I use my favourite no-churn ice-cream recipe in these ice-cream sandwiches which makes them really quick and easy. You could use your own favourite ice-cream; just defrost it slightly so you can spread it between the brownie layers easily.

MAKES 12 LARGE SANDWICHES

1 x My Favourite Brownie recipe (page 106)
200ml condensed milk
600ml double cream
1 tsp vanilla bean paste
100g Oreos, or biscuit of your choice

You will also need two or three 20 x 30cm brownie tins and an electric hand-held whisk.

1. Line one 20 x 30cm tin with cling film.

2. In a large bowl, whisk together the condensed milk, double cream and vanilla using an electric hand-held whisk until the mixture thickens and holds its shape when you take the whisk out. Put the biscuits into a plastic bag and bash them with a rolling pin to make crumbs. If you want larger chunks, you could crumble them by hand. Fold the biscuit crumbs into the ice-cream mixture, then scrape into the prepared tin. Use a spatula to smooth it out, then freeze for at least two hours or until firm.

3. Preheat the oven to 180°C/160°C fan/gas 4. Make My Favourite Brownie recipe up to step 4, but don't put the mixture in the tin yet.

4. Divide the brownie mixture between two lined 20 x 30cm brownie tins (or use one and bake two batches) and use a spatula to spread the batter right into the edges. It will be very thin, as these will be your sandwich layers. Bake each tray for ten minutes, then remove from the oven and leave to cool completely in the tin.

5. Remove the brownie layers from the tins and re-line one of the tins with another sheet of baking parchment. Put one brownie layer into the tin, then press the ice-cream layer on the top of it. Add the final layer then return to the freezer for at least 30 minutes.

6. Remove the ice-cream sandwich slab from the freezer about ten minutes before serving. Use a sharp knife or pastry cutter to cut shapes – I like the effect of a circular cutter.

BROWNIE IN A MUG

This is a recipe for those moments where you absolutely must have a brownie, straight away! I've listed the measurements in spoonfuls to make it super quick – you don't even need scales.

MAKES 2 MUGFULS

3 tbsp butter
2 tbsp light brown sugar
3 tbsp caster sugar
2 tbsp cocoa powder
1 egg
2 tbsp plain flour
1 tbsp dark chocolate chips
Whipped cream and chocolate shavings, to decorate

1. In a large, microwaveable mug, mix together the butter and sugars. Microwave on high for one minute, making sure to stir halfway through. The sugar and butter will start to melt together.

2. Leave the sugar to cool for a few minutes, then beat in the cocoa powder followed by the egg. Fold in the flour gently; you don't want too much gluten developing, because it will over-rise and be tough, not chewy.

3. Transfer half of the mixture into another mug or ramekin (you can refrigerate this and microwave it later or share with a friend!), then sprinkle the chocolate chips over the top of both.

4. Microwave on high for 30 seconds. The brownie will rise and fall a bit while it is cooking and should still be slightly gooey when done. Leave to stand for a few minutes to allow the heat to disperse evenly before enjoying with a large scoop of ice-cream! You could bake this in the oven instead of the microwave at 180°C/160°C fan/gas 4 for five minutes to get the crisp top; just make sure that the mug is ovenproof.

5. Serve with a big dollop of whipped cream and chocolate shavings, then get stuck in with a spoon!

REGGAE ROAD

This twist on a rocky road is an unusual tropical version: a sweet white chocolate bar packed with juicy rum-soaked pineapple, ginger biscuits and banana chips.

MAKES 14 BARS

100g unsweetened dried
  pineapple, chopped
5 tbsp white rum or Malibu
300g white chocolate,
  chopped into even-sized
  pieces
100g ginger biscuits
50g desiccated coconut
25g dried banana chips
50g mini marshmallows

TO DECORATE
20g dried banana chips,
  chopped
1 tbsp palm sugar
2 tbsp desiccated coconut

You will also need a
20 x 30cm brownie tin.

1. Line a 20 x 30cm tin with baking parchment.

2. Put the dried pineapple into into a small bowl. Pour over three tablespoons of the rum and leave to soak – this can take between 30 minutes and two hours, or can be done in the fridge overnight. It is not a necessary step, but it really enhances the flavour of the finished bake.

3. Put the white chocolate into a heatproof bowl over a saucepan of barely simmering water, stirring now and again to stop it burning. White chocolate is difficult to melt properly, so make sure you keep the heat low and avoid steam getting into the mixture as this will make the chocolate seize and go grainy. I find the best way to do this is to put the chocolate into a small plastic container with a lid and leave it to stand in boiling water. The chocolate takes 5–7 minutes to melt fully. When the chocolate has nearly melted, take the pan off the heat but leave the bowl over the water for a few more minutes, stirring until it is smooth.

4. Add the remaining rum a teaspoon at a time to the white chocolate, stirring after each addition. Initially the mixture will seize and turn lumpy, but after three or four spoonfuls it should become smooth. As soon as the mixture turns smooth, stop adding the rum – you may not need it all. If you add too much, the bars will not set properly.

5. Break the biscuits into small pieces and stir into the chocolate with the soaked pineapple, coconut, banana chips and marshmallows until they are all completely coated. Pour into the prepared tin and push the mixture right into the edges. Sprinkle the chopped banana chips, palm sugar and coconut over the top, then put into the fridge for at least two hours before slicing with a sharp knife. It should set into firm bars. Store in the fridge, where it will keep for up to two weeks.

ROUTE 66 ROCKY ROAD

Having been lucky enough to travel to the US a few times, it is only right to include some of my favourite American flavours – peanuts, popcorn, marshmallows and cranberries – in my version of rocky road. Marshmallows, syrup and chocolate make a soft, sweet base, cut with the welcome sharpness of cranberries and peanuts.

MAKES 12 BARS

100g butter
100g peanut butter
200g dark chocolate, chopped
100g milk chocolate, chopped
2 tbsp golden syrup
50g peanuts
50g dried cranberries
50g mini marshmallows
50g toffee popcorn

You will also need a 20 x 30cm baking tin.

1. Line a 20 x 30cm tin with baking parchment.

2. In a large heatproof bowl set over a pan of simmering water, melt the butter, peanut butter and both chocolates together until they are smooth. Stir in the golden syrup.

3. Roughly chop the peanuts and mix them with the cranberries, mini marshmallows and popcorn. Add these dry ingredients to the chocolate and mix to combine. Make sure all the popcorn is well coated in chocolate or the rocky road won't stick together.

4. Press the mixture into the tin using the back of a spatula or wooden spoon, then chill in the fridge for at least two hours to set.

5. Use a sharp knife to slice it into 12 bars. To keep it as solid as possible, store in the fridge until ready to eat. It will keep for up to two weeks.

BOLLYWOOD BAR

I first tasted this delicious version of rocky road in a bakery in Southwold. It's not where you might expect to encounter Bollywood-themed bakes, but it was a happy surprise discovery for me. This is my attempt to do justice to the flavours of India which that Suffolk bakery managed so well.

MAKES 14 BARS OR 28 SMALL SQUARES

300g white chocolate
25g butter, cubed
8 cardamom pods or ½ tsp ground cardamom
½ tsp chilli powder
125g digestive biscuits
50g pistachio nuts
50g dried apricots, chopped
50g mini marshmallows

TO DECORATE
10 pistachio nuts, chopped
4 dried apricots, chopped

You will also need a 20 x 30cm brownie tin.

1. Line a 20 x 30cm tin with baking parchment.

2. Chop the white chocolate into small cubes that are all roughly the same size and put into a heatproof bowl with the butter. Put the bowl over a saucepan of barely simmering water, stirring now and again to stop it burning. White chocolate is difficult to melt properly, so make sure you keep the heat low and avoid steam getting into the mixture as this will make the chocolate seize and go grainy. When the chocolate has nearly melted, take the pan off the heat but leave the bowl over the water for a few more minutes, stirring until it is smooth.

3. Split the cardamom pods (if using), empty out the seeds and discard the pods then crush the seeds in a pestle and mortar. If you don't have a pestle and mortar, put the seeds into a plastic bag and use a rolling pin to crush them to a powder. Add the ground cardamom and the chilli to the melted chocolate and stir.

4. Break the biscuits into small pieces and stir into the chocolate with the pistachio nuts, dried apricots and marshmallows until they are all completely coated. Pour into the prepared tin and push the mixture right into the edges. Sprinkle the chopped pistachio nuts and apricot pieces over the top, then put into the fridge for at least two hours before slicing. Store in the fridge, where it will keep for up to two weeks.

SESAME SNAP BLONDIES

I love sesame snap biscuits; there is something about the way they weld your mouth together with sticky caramel and the seeds get stuck between your teeth that is surprisingly enjoyable. These blondies are a grown-up version of my much-loved childhood snack. If you can't get hold of tahini, blitz some toasted sesame seeds in a food processor until they release their oils and turn into a thick paste.

MAKES 12 SQUARES

150g butter, plus extra for greasing
350g light brown sugar
2 eggs
75g tahini paste
200g plain flour
½ tsp baking powder
50g sesame seeds
4 tbsp runny honey

You will also need a 25 x 30cm brownie tin.

1. Preheat the oven to 200°C/180°C fan/gas 6. Grease a 25 x 30cm tin and line with baking parchment.

2. In a large saucepan, heat the butter and the brown sugar together until the butter has completely melted. Remove from the heat and allow to cool to room temperature – if you don't allow the mixture to cool, the eggs will scramble when you add them.

3. Beat the eggs into the cooled mixture using a wooden spoon then fold in the tahini. Sift over the flour and baking powder, and mix until well combined. Scrape into the tin and sprinkle over the sesame seeds, trying to get an even covering.

4. Bake for 25–30 minutes then allow to cool completely in the tin. Blondies take a few hours to firm up, so chill in the fridge or freezer if you are in a hurry.

5. When they are cool, spoon the honey into a heatproof bowl and microwave for 30 seconds to make it easier to spread. Drizzle the warm honey over the top of the blondies before cutting into squares. Store in an airtight container for up to one week.

TWIST: STEM GINGER BLONDIES

For a gingerbread kick, replace the tahini with 4 tablespoons of ginger syrup from a jar of stem ginger. Finely chop two balls of stem ginger and stir into the batter before baking as above. Leave out the sesame seeds.

Melt 100g white chocolate and drizzle over the finished blondie instead of honey, and decorate with small pieces of crystallised ginger.

MY FAVOURITE FLAPJACKS

A flapjack is always one of my go-to bakes if I am in a hurry. My recipe is a one-pan method, which means minimal mess, and with only four ingredients, it is one of the simplest recipes in this book.

Despite being so easy to rustle up, the satisfaction gained from a perfectly chewy, buttery flapjack is that of something far more complex. Try adding different dried fruits and toppings to make this classic recipe even more special.

**MAKES ABOUT
12 LARGE SQUARES**

150g butter, plus extra for
  greasing
125g demerara sugar
1 tbsp golden syrup
225g rolled oats

You will also need a
20 x 30cm brownie tin.

1. Preheat the oven to 200°C/180°C fan/gas 6. Grease a 20 x 30cm tin and line with baking parchment.

2. Put the butter, sugar and syrup into a large heavy-based saucepan. Heat the mixture gently, stirring occasionally, until the butter has completely melted and the sugar has almost dissolved.

3. Mix the oats into the hot sugar and butter, and stir together until all the oats are completely coated.

4. Turn the mixture into the prepared tin and use the back of a spatula to press it down into an even layer.

5. For soft and chewy flapjacks, bake for 15 minutes so the top has just started to caramelise and is a light golden colour. For crunchy flapjacks, bake for a further ten minutes.

6. Leave to cool for five minutes in the tin, then use a sharp knife to mark into bars or squares. The flapjacks will keep in an airtight container for up to ten days.

STICKY TOFFEE FLAPJACKS

The black treacle in this gooey flapjack is reminiscent of, in my opinion, the best dessert in the world: sticky toffee pudding. The thick caramel sauce and toasted pecans make this flapjack the ultimate treat – it's a real crowd pleaser!

MAKES ABOUT 12 LARGE SQUARES

1 x My Favourite Flapjacks recipe (opposite)
1 tbsp black treacle
150g Medjool dates, destoned and quartered

TOFFEE TOPPING

100g dark brown sugar
25g butter
1 tbsp golden syrup
2 tbsp double cream
50g toasted pecans

You will also need a 20 x 30cm brownie tin.

1. Make My Favourite Flapjacks recipe, swapping black treacle for the golden syrup, up to step 3.

2. Mix the dates into the flapjack base. Press into the prepared tin, smoothing it over with a spatula to get an even layer, then bake for 15 minutes. This flapjack is darker than most, so be careful not to overbake it: you want the flapjack to be sticky and soft. Allow to cool completely in the tin.

3. To make the topping, put the dark brown sugar, butter and golden syrup into a small saucepan and bring to the boil. Stirring all the time, cook the mixture for five minutes or until thickened and bubbling. Carefully stir in the double cream and allow to cool slightly.

4. Roughly chop half the toasted pecans, then drizzle the toffee sauce over the flapjack. Sprinkle on the whole and chopped nuts and leave to set for about 30 minutes, or until the toffee sauce has cooled, before slicing into squares. The flapjacks will keep in an airtight container for up to ten days.

MILLIONAIRE'S FLAPJACK

To get a really shiny, professional top, I recommend tempering the chocolate for the topping (see how on page 208), but if you are short of time it will still taste the same without this step.

**MAKES ABOUT
15 BARS**

1 x My Favourite Flapjacks
recipe (page 120)

CARAMEL
150g butter
1 x 397g tin condensed milk
100g golden syrup

TOPPING
300g dark chocolate,
chopped
50g white chocolate,
chopped

You will also need a
20 x 30cm brownie tin.

1. Make My Favourite Flapjacks recipe up to step 5, baking it for 20 minutes so the flapjack is crunchy and firm enough to be a sturdy base. Allow to cool completely in the tin.

2. To make the caramel, put the butter, condensed milk and golden syrup into a medium saucepan and heat gently, stirring until the butter has melted. Bring the mixture to the boil and continue to stir until it turns golden brown. Allow to cool for a few minutes before pouring it over the cooled flapjack. Leave to set and cool completely.

3. In a heatproof bowl set over a pan of simmering water, melt the dark chocolate until it is smooth and pourable. Melt the white chocolate and put it into a piping bag – if the piping bag is microwave safe, I often cheat by putting chunks of white chocolate straight into it then microwaving the bag and chocolate in 15-second bursts until the chocolate has melted.

4. Pour the dark chocolate over the set caramel and tilt the tray so it covers the whole flapjack. Before the dark chocolate sets, snip the tip off the piping bag and pipe the white chocolate in large swirls all over the top.

5. Leave to set at room temperature, then use a sharp knife to divide into 15 bars. The flapjacks will keep in an airtight container for up to ten days.

SWEET DOUGH

LIME → orange ← LEMON
CURD

APRICOT

Raspberry ← JAM

BLACKCURRANT

FRUITY filling

Lemon
MOUSSE
SUMMER BERRY

vanilla
COFFEE | CHOCOLATE
CUSTARD

EVOLUTION OF THE DOUGHNUT

WHITE
MILK | DARK
CHOCOLATE GANACHE

CREAMY filling

DECADENT filling

FRESH CREAM

CINNAMON liqueur

CARAMEL
DULCE DE LECHE | salted

DOUGHNUTS

If you can make bread, you can make doughnuts.

They aren't as hard as people think – they just require a close eye and a lot of patience. The dough is very similar to simple bread dough, but it has been enriched by the addition of milk, butter and eggs, which give it a much softer texture. Adding these ingredients has an effect on how the dough rises and how long it takes to bake, so you need to be aware of what each one does.

Sugar and fats found in butter, milk and egg yolks can all interfere with gluten development; because when flour gets coated in fat it struggles to form gluten as readily. This can make the dough a little trickier to work with. Due to the added fat, the dough will feel different when you knead it. It will be heavier and stickier, but try not to add too much more flour to it. Instead, oil the work surface and persevere in kneading until the dough eventually turns smooth and stretchy. The dough also takes longer to rise, so be patient and wait for it to double in size or the resulting bread will be too dense.

Once cooked, the gorgeous soft pillows can be filled with anything from fresh cream to fruity mousses – they are a great versatile base for trying out new things. To create even more of a flavour sensation, you can also roll the filled doughnuts in freeze-dried fruit powders, infused sugars or even sherbet.

MY FAVOURITE DOUGHNUTS

Homemade doughnuts are more delicious than anything you can buy in the shops. They are best eaten warm, fresh from the pan and rolled in crunchy sugar; in my house they disappear as fast as I fry them!

MAKES 16

100g unsalted butter, cubed
150ml whole milk
2 eggs
500g strong white bread
    flour
1 tsp salt
14g fast action dried yeast
60g caster sugar
Sunflower oil, around
    2 litres, for deep-frying

1. Place the butter in a small saucepan with the milk. Heat very gently over a low heat until the butter has melted completely and the milk is warmed through. Meanwhile, beat the eggs together in a small jug.

2. Put the flour into a large mixing bowl, and add the salt to one side of the bowl and the yeast to the other. This positioning is important, because salt can kill yeast if you put it right on top of it, which will stop your dough from rising. Tip the sugar into the bowl and make a well in the middle of the flour mixture.

3. Pour the warm milk and butter and the beaten eggs into the well in the flour and stir the mixture together using a round-ended knife or a wooden spoon. Keep mixing until all the flour is incorporated and a soft, sticky dough forms.

4. Lightly oil a clean work surface and tip the dough out onto it. Knead for 5–10 minutes, or until it is no longer sticky and forms a smooth ball. It should spring back if you poke it with your finger – this shows that you have developed enough gluten. Put it in a lightly oiled bowl, cover with cling film or a clean tea towel and leave to rise for at least one hour at room temperature or until doubled in size.

5. Tip the risen dough out onto a work surface and fold it in on itself a few times to knock out any large air bubbles. Divide into 16 evenly sized pieces and form into small balls by rolling each piece in cupped hands to smooth the surface all over. Arrange on an oiled tray loosely covered with cling film and leave for 30–45 minutes or until noticeably larger.

6. In a large heavy-based saucepan, heat the oil to 160°C. If the oil is too hot, the doughnuts will brown too quickly on the outside and still be raw in the middle. If it is not hot enough, the dough will absorb too much oil and will be greasy. If you don't have a thermometer, try dropping a small piece of bread into the oil – it should sizzle when it comes into contact with the oil, but take a few minutes to brown.

7. Deep-fry the doughnuts in batches of two or three at a time, cooking for 2–3 minutes on each side until golden brown before removing them with a slotted spoon and placing on a tray lined with kitchen paper to soak up any excess oil. Don't let the oil get too hot at any stage, or you will get irregular doughnuts that are not cooked properly. I use a thermometer to monitor the oil for the whole frying process.

8. Fill and roll your doughnuts in whatever you like – try my lemon sherbet or crème brûlée fillings on the following pages. Homemade doughnuts are best eaten as soon as they are made, or at least on the same day.

CRÈME BRÛLÉE DOUGHNUTS

One of the best doughnuts I have ever eaten was from a little café in Piccadilly tube station. The outside shattered when you bit your teeth into it, and the fluffy dough contained a vanilla-specked custard filling. This is my version, a nifty hand-held crème brûlée.

MAKES 16

1 x My Favourite Doughnuts recipe (pages 128–129)

CRÈME PÂTISSIÈRE
350ml whole milk
1 tsp vanilla bean paste
4 egg yolks
30g cornflour
75g caster sugar
40g unsalted butter, softened

CARAMEL TOPPING
250g caster sugar

You will also need an electric hand-held whisk.

1. Start by making the crème pâtissière. In a small saucepan, heat the milk and vanilla bean paste together over a low heat until steaming and almost boiling.

2. Use an electric hand-held whisk to beat together the egg yolks, cornflour and caster sugar in a heatproof jug until a thick paste forms. Whisk until the mixture has turned a slightly lighter colour.

3. When the milk is steaming, pour a small amount into the egg mixture and quickly whisk it in. If you aren't quick enough, the hot milk will scramble the egg. Gradually add the rest of the hot milk, whisking all the time, until it is all incorporated.

4. Pour the custard back into the saucepan and continue to heat, still whisking all the time, until it becomes a very thick paste. This can happen very suddenly, because as soon as the eggs get to the right temperature they set and thicken the mixture. Transfer to a jug, stir in the butter, then cover with cling film and chill for at least one hour or until cool.

5. Make My Favourite Doughnuts recipe, then use a skewer to make a hole in the side of each cooked doughnut and wiggle it around to hollow out the middle.

6. Fit a piping bag with a special long nozzle designed for filling doughnuts, or cut a small hole in the tip of a disposable one. Spoon in the chilled crème pâtissière and fill each doughnut through the hole. Allow the doughnuts to stand on their side so the filling can settle before laying them down on a piece of baking parchment.

7. For the topping, put the sugar into a saucepan and heat gently until it has started to melt. Allow the sugar to turn a golden caramel colour, then pour the caramel over the doughnuts. It will harden as it cools which will create the crack you expect from crème brûlée. To make it even more authentic, you could use a blowtorch to brown the top of the caramel even more once it has hardened, but they will taste just as good with or without this step.

LEMON SHERBET DOUGHNUTS

If you haven't got time to make the lemon mousse, you could use a simple Lemon Curd (see page 21), but the mousse does add a lightness that makes the doughnut experience a little less stodgy! I dust these in zingy sherbet, which gives them a great sour flavour.

MAKES 16

1 x My Favourite Doughnuts recipe (pages 128–129)

LEMON MOUSSE
2 eggs, separated
125g caster sugar
Zest and juice of 2 unwaxed lemons
2 tsp powdered gelatine
150ml double cream

SHERBET COATING
100g icing sugar
2 sherbet fountain sweets, or 50g sherbet powder

You will also need an electric hand-held whisk.

1. To make the lemon mousse, put the egg whites into a clean, grease-free small bowl and whisk using an electric hand-held whisk until soft peaks form. You don't want them to be too stiff or it will be difficult to fold them into the mousse later.

2. In a large bowl, use the same whisk (don't worry about cleaning it) to mix the egg yolks, caster sugar, lemon zest and juice until the sugar has dissolved and the mixture has slightly thickened. This takes about five minutes.

3. Put 3 tablespoons of hot water into a small jug, sprinkle over the gelatine, and stir until the gelatine has melted.

4. Whip the cream into soft peaks in a separate bowl, then stir in the warm gelatine mix.

5. Fold the whipped cream into the egg yolk mixture using a large metal spoon until it is completely combined. Gently fold in the whipped egg whites, and when no large lumps remain and the mixture has thickened, pour into a large bowl and refrigerate for at least one hour or until set.

6. Sift the icing sugar into a bowl that is big enough to accommodate a doughnut comfortably. Set the liquorice sticks aside for later then empty the sherbet fountains into the sieve and sift into the bowl with the icing sugar. Or just add the sherbet powder to the sugar.

7. Make My Favourite Doughnuts recipe.

8. Use a skewer to pierce the side of each cooked doughnut, and wiggle it around to make a hole inside big enough to hold the filling.

9. Roll each doughnut in the sherbet sugar until completely coated. You might have to repeat this two or three times to get an even coverage. I find it easiest to stand the doughnuts up on their side in a square tin after they are coated so the filling doesn't seep out when I fill them.

10. Gently spoon the lemon mousse into a disposable piping bag and cut a small hole in the tip. Fill each doughnut with mousse and leave them to sit for at least 30 minutes so the mousse can firm up again. I like to chop the liquorice stick from the sherbet fountain into small pieces and stick one into the end of each doughnut where the hole is, but this is optional. Eat them quickly; they're much better fresh!

ICED RING DOUGHNUTS

I think ring doughnuts are a really fun bake, probably due to their cartoon associations. They can be as colourful as you like, left plain or decorated with sprinkles. I use pastel colours and feathered icing on mine to make them look a little like giant party ring biscuits! Use fondant icing sugar in the icing if you can get your hands on it – it sets more firmly and has a better consistency.

MAKES 18

1 x My Favourite Doughnuts recipe (pages 128–129)

TOPPING
350g fondant icing sugar or icing sugar
Assortment of gel food colourings

1. Make My Favourite Doughnuts recipe up to step 5. To make ring doughnuts instead of round ones, roll the dough out into a large rectangle around 2cm thick and use a 9cm round cutter to cut as many circles as you can. Use a 4cm round cutter to punch a hole out of the centre of each dough circle. Re-roll the remaining dough and repeat the cutting process. Arrange on an oiled tray loosely covered with cling film and leave at room temperature for 30–45 minutes or until noticeably larger.

2. Fry as described in step 6 of the doughnut recipe, but as these are rings they will only take two minutes on each side. Drain on kitchen paper to soak up the excess oil.

3. To make the icing, place the sugar into a bowl and mix with 2–3 tablespoons of cold water until a fairly thick paste forms. You want it to be thick enough to run off the spoon in a slow stream and not remain in a lump; add a little more water if necessary. You can play around with the icing as you go – if it doesn't stick to the doughnuts, add a little more water, and if it runs off the edges too quickly, add more sugar.

4. Divide the white icing between three bowls large enough to fit one doughnut and use a toothpick to add a tiny amount of gel food colouring to each bowl. Stir in the food colouring until you have reached the desired shade. I tend to leave one white, and colour the other two yellow and pink. If you want to create a party ring effect, place a tablespoon of each icing colour into piping bags.

5. Dip the doughnuts face down into one colour of icing and wiggle them around so the top is completely coated before lifting out. Allow excess icing to drip back into the bowl, then twist the doughnut in your hand while turning it back over to get a clean edge. If you're making party rings, pipe a few horizontal lines of icing across the doughnut then drag a toothpick through the icing to feather it. Place on a cooling rack to set.

CHOCOLATE AND LIME FUNNEL CAKES

Funnel cakes are a type of non-yeasted doughnut, often found at fairgrounds in North America. They are really quick to make, and their swirly pattern is unusual and eye-catching. I taught a group of young girls in a village in Cambodia how to make these when I visited the country with the charity Tearfund. I was learning about the horrors of child trafficking; the girls I met were vulnerable and living in extreme poverty, which made them prime targets for traffickers. Equipping them with one skill – whether that be sewing, motorbike repair or even cooking these little cakes – can be life-changing, as they then have the ability to generate an income which allows them to stay safe at home with their families. That makes this recipe so special to me, demonstrating that something as simple as a cake can change the world, one small step at a time.

MAKES 4–6

1 large egg
1 tsp vanilla extract
100ml whole milk
Zest of 2 unwaxed limes
100g plain flour
1 tsp baking powder
1 tbsp caster sugar
Pinch of salt
100g caster sugar, to dust
Vegetable oil, for frying

CHOCOLATE SAUCE
150g dark chocolate,
    chopped
100ml double cream
2 tbsp golden syrup

1. In a small jug, whisk together the egg, vanilla, milk and half the lime zest.
2. Combine the flour, baking powder, tablespoon of caster sugar and salt in a small bowl. Make a well in the centre before whisking in the wet ingredients, mixing until there are no lumps remaining. You should have a thick custardy batter. Pour into a disposable piping bag.
3. In a small saucepan, heat around 3cm of oil until it sizzles if you sprinkle in a pinch of flour.
4. Snip the tip off the piping bag. Squeeze about a sixth of the batter into the oil, in a spiral, starting at the edges and filling the circle with a random, wiggly pattern.
5. Cook for about one minute until the edges start to brown, then flip it over and cook for two minutes more on the other side. It should be an even, golden brown colour on both sides.
6. Remove and cool on kitchen paper then dust with sugar mixed with the remaining lime zest. Repeat the frying process with the remaining mixture.
7. For the chocolate sauce, put the chocolate in a saucepan with the cream and golden syrup. Heat gently, stirring all the time, until all the chocolate has melted. Drizzle over the funnel cakes, or use as a dip. These are best served hot and fresh.

MY FAVOURITE ENRICHED DOUGH

Any dough that has had oil, butter, eggs or sugar added to it is known as an enriched dough. Brioche, cinnamon buns and pretzels are all made with enriched doughs. You can read more about what affect these additions have on your dough on page 127.

These doughs have a delicate texture and are really moist and tender. They are a little trickier to work with and take longer to rise, but it is worth it for the soft, flavoursome crumb that you will get.

MAKES ENOUGH DOUGH FOR ONE LARGE LOAF OR 12 MEDIUM-SIZED BUNS

75g unsalted butter, cubed
200ml whole milk
500g strong plain flour
7g fast action dried yeast
1 tsp salt
50g caster sugar
2 eggs

1. Put the butter into a small saucepan with the milk. Heat on low until the cubes of butter are completely melted, then set to one side to allow the mixture to cool for a few minutes.

2. Put the flour into a large bowl and add the yeast to one side of the bowl and the salt and sugar to the other. This positioning is important, because if you put the salt directly onto the yeast it may kill it, which will stop your dough from rising.

3. Beat the eggs into the lukewarm milk mixture (it should feel slightly warm when you stick a finger into it). Gradually add this to the dry ingredients, stirring all the time, until a sticky but not wet dough forms. You may not need to add all the milk mixture.

4. Turn the dough out onto a lightly oiled work surface and knead for 10–15 minutes, or until it is no longer sticky and has become a smooth and elastic dough. Put it into an oiled bowl, cover with cling film and leave in a warm place for 1–2 hours or until doubled in size.

5. When the dough has risen, turn it out onto the oiled surface and fold it in on itself a couple of times to knock out any large air bubbles. Your dough is now ready for shaping.

PRETZEL STICKS AND DIPS

Pretzel sticks are a great thing to make when friends or family come over. Put them out on a big platter with a few dips for people to mix and match – Gingerbread Caramel, fiery Chilli Chocolate and Peanut Butter and Blackcurrant are always popular (see pages 141 and 143)!

It feels very odd to throw your carefully proofed dough into boiling water, but this gives pretzels and bagels their soft and chewy texture. If you leave this step out, you will create breadsticks not pretzels. Boiling the dough cooks the outside of the bread, stopping it rising too much when baked and creating a denser, chewier centre.

MAKES 30 STICKS

1 x My Favourite Enriched
  Dough recipe (page 138)
3 tbsp bicarbonate of soda
1 egg, beaten

1. Make My Favourite Enriched Dough recipe and roll the dough out into a large rectangle.

2. Preheat the oven to 220°C/200°C fan/gas 7 and line two large baking sheets with baking parchment. Slice the dough in half, then divide into 30 even strips (15 strips from each half). Roll each one between your hands to make it more rounded then put onto another baking sheet or a large plate. You will have to cook these sticks in batches, so cover with a clean tea towel until needed.

3. Measure 1.5 litres of water into a saucepan and bring to the boil. When the water is boiling, add the bicarbonate of soda and stir until it stops fizzing. Turn the heat down and leave at a low simmer.

4. Put the dough sticks into the saucepan and boil for around 30 seconds each. Remove from the water and put them on a piece of kitchen paper to dry off the excess water before putting them on one of the lined baking sheets.

5. Brush the beaten egg over the sticks, then bake for 7–8 minutes or until golden brown all over. I bake these in batches, baking one whilst boiling the next.

6. When the sticks come out of the oven, leave them to cool briefly before moving them onto a cooling rack. These are best served hot from the oven, dipped in one of the combinations on pages 141 and 143.

CINNAMON SUGAR

COATS 12 STICKS

1 tbsp butter
1 tsp ground cinnamon
50g caster sugar

1. Melt the butter then use a pastry brush to coat each stick with it. Mix together the cinnamon and sugar, then sprinkle over the buttered sticks.

GINGERBREAD CARAMEL DIP

200g caster sugar
25g butter
50ml double cream
½ tsp ground ginger
½ tsp ground cinnamon
¼ tsp ground nutmeg

1. Put the caster sugar into a large, heavy-based saucepan. Add 4 tablespoons of water and stir until the sugar and water are well mixed. Bring to a low simmer and cook gently until it turns brown. Don't stir at this point or the sugar will crystallise and you will have to start again! You want the caramel to be a light amber colour, reading at around 165°C on a sugar thermometer, if you have one.

2. As soon as the caramel is the right colour, take the pan off the heat and stir in the butter. It will splutter and spit, so be careful. When the sauce is smooth, add the cream and spices and mix until combined. Store in a sealed container in the fridge for up to two weeks then, when you want to use it, microwave it gently.

PEANUT BUTTER AND BLACKCURRANT DIP

100g full-fat cream cheese
1 tbsp icing sugar
100g smooth peanut butter
3 tbsp blackcurrant jam or curd

1. In a small saucepan, melt the cream cheese and icing sugar together. Stir in the peanut butter then, when the mixture is smooth, pour into a small ramekin.

2. Swirl the jam or curd through the dip, then get stuck in with the pretzel sticks! It will keep for up to one week in a sealed container in the fridge.

CHILLI CHOCOLATE DIP

75ml double cream
½ tsp chilli powder
Zest of ½ an unwaxed orange
100g dark chocolate, chopped

1. Put the cream into a small saucepan and add the chilli powder and orange zest. Heat on medium until the cream just begins to steam, then remove from the heat and stir in the chocolate.

2. Mix until there are no lumps of chocolate left; if there are any that refuse to melt, return to the heat, stirring until they disappear. Pour into a ramekin and enjoy with the pretzels as a chocolate dip with a kick. It will keep for up to one week in a sealed container in the fridge.

CINNAMON BUNS WITH CREAM CHEESE ICING

When I was little, my mum occasionally used to take my sister and me to a theme park close to where we live. At the exit there was a stall where they baked fresh cinnamon rolls, and the smell of warm spice would prevent anyone from leaving empty-handed. We'd eat the giant rolls instead of dinner, then again for breakfast, and soon I learnt to bake them myself. It still remains one of my family's favourite recipes. You can make individual rolls or bake them together in a tin so they become a tear-and-share bread.

MAKES 8 LARGE ROLLS

1 x My Favourite Enriched Dough recipe (page 138)
200g soft brown sugar
2 tsp ground cinnamon
50g butter, at room temperature, plus extra for greasing
1 egg, beaten

CREAM CHEESE ICING
50g full-fat cream cheese
25g butter, at room temperature
150g icing sugar

You will also need a 23cm round tin.

1. Make My Favourite Enriched Dough recipe and, once risen, roll the dough into a large rectangle about 40cm long and as wide as possible. The thinner you can roll the dough, the more delicious cinnamon filling you can get into the buns.

2. In a small bowl, combine the brown sugar and the cinnamon until they are evenly mixed. Spread the soft butter all over the dough then sprinkle the cinnamon sugar over the top of it. Press the sugar into the dough using your hands to get an even layer. When it covers the whole rectangle, tightly roll the dough, starting from the 40cm side. Roll it towards you to make a long sausage.

3. Slice off the ends of the sausage so you can see the spiral, which will make all the buns look the same. You can still bake the offcuts, if you like! Slice the rest crossways into eight 5cm rolls and put them into a greased circular 23cm round tin, packing them in close. If you want to make individual buns, put them onto a lined baking sheet with enough space for them to double in size. Cover the buns with oiled cling film and leave to double in size – this will take 45 minutes to 1 hour.

4. Preheat the oven to 200°C/180°C fan/gas 6. Brush the risen buns with the beaten egg and bake for 15–20 minutes or until golden brown. The sugar should have melted and will be bubbling over.

5. To make the cream cheese icing, beat the cream cheese and soft butter together in a small bowl until well combined. Add the icing sugar and mix until a thick paste forms.

6. Drip the icing over the warm cinnamon buns, spreading it with the back of a spoon to get an even coating. Serve immediately when warm, or reheat in the oven the following day to refresh the dough.

TWIST: CINNAMON SWIRL LOAF

1. Make the cinnamon bun recipe opposite into one large loaf with a spiral centre. You can even mix raisins or dried fruit into the dough for an extra treat. Line a 1.5-litre loaf tin with baking parchment. It seems unusual to line a bread tin, but it will stop the loaf from sticking if any sugar leaks out.

2. Roll the dough out into a rectangle, with the short side of the dough the same length as the long side of the tin. Spread the butter, sugar and cinnamon over the dough, the same way as opposite. Roll up tightly into a coil and pinch the ends together before placing into the loaf tin. Cover and leave to rise for one hour, or until the dough is peeping over the top of the tin.

3. Preheat the oven to 200°C/180°C fan/gas 6. Brush the top of the loaf with the beaten egg and put into the centre of the oven. Bake for 20 minutes, or until the top is dark and glossy and sounds hollow when tapped. Allow to cool for a few minutes in the tin before turning out onto a cooling rack and leave to cool completely before slicing.

CHRISTMAS MORNING BUNS

These buns are a festive twist on a Chelsea bun. I think the mincemeat filling makes a welcome change from a classic mince pie and, shaped like a Christmas tree, this is a great Christmas centrepiece perfect for sharing.

MAKES 11 ROLLS

1 x My Favourite Enriched
    Dough recipe (page 138)
1 x 410g jar mincemeat
50g caster sugar
75g marzipan, chopped into
    small pieces
Zest and juice of 1 unwaxed
    orange
1 egg, beaten
50g smooth marmalade
50g icing sugar
Glacé cherries (optional)

1. Make My Favourite Enriched Dough recipe and, once risen, roll it into a large rectangle about 45cm long.

2. Spread the mincemeat over the dough in an even layer, then cover with the caster sugar. Sprinkle the marzipan over the mincemeat, followed by the orange zest.

3. Starting with the 45cm side, roll the dough towards you into a long sausage shape. Slice off the ends of the sausage so you can see the spiral, which will make all the buns look the same. You can still bake the offcuts, if you like! Cut into 11 equal-sized rolls and put onto a lined baking sheet in a tree formation – 1, 2, 3, 4, 1. Cover with oiled cling film and leave to rise for 45 minutes to 1 hour, until almost doubled in size.

4. Preheat the oven to 200°C/180°C fan/gas 6. Brush the buns with the beaten egg then bake for 20 minutes, or until the top is golden brown and the buns have risen.

5. Heat the marmalade in a small saucepan until liquid, then brush over the buns to create a sticky glaze.

6. Mix the icing sugar with the orange juice so it forms a thick paste. Put into an piping bag and pipe lines across the bread, following the natural line between each row of buns to create a tinsel effect. You could even add glacé cherry baubles, if you like. Serve warm for the freshest flavour.

PASTRY

CHOUX PASTRY

Choux pastry is my favourite kind of pastry to make, and not just because it is responsible for many delicious things like éclairs, profiteroles and even mightier structures like tall towers of choux buns stuck together with caramel.

CHOUX PASTRY SCIENCE

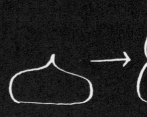

UNBAKED
CHOUX DOUGH

FIRST 10 MINUTES
OF BAKING

← SET
OUTSIDE

Hollow middle

CRISP HOLLOW
CHOUX BUNS

I find it amazing that what looks like a gloopy, sticky dough can utterly transform in the oven into crisp, hollow, golden buns. The method is unlike any other pastry, with no rolling or folding involved, and it is easier than you might think.

The most important thing about choux pastry is not the flour, or the eggs, but the water. Or rather the steam that water becomes. When ingredients like water, milk and eggs are heated, the water in them turns into steam. All baked goods rely on steam for some of their rise, as all baked goods contain a liquid of some kind that can evaporate. Choux pastry has a high water content and, in the oven, the steam expands inside the pastry, the egg proteins begin to stretch and the pastry puffs out. Eventually, most of the protein structure breaks, but due to the high heat the outside has already set, so the characteristic hollow middle is formed.

In most pastries, gluten development is kept to a minimum to prevent it from being tough and chewy. With choux pastry the opposite is true; it needs a strong gluten structure to hold its shape once baked so I use half strong bread flour, which contains more gluten, to strengthen the pastry.

Finally, it is important to bake choux pastry properly until completely dry. If any steam is left inside the buns when they are removed from the oven, it will condense back into water, making the pastry soggy and prone to collapse. To prevent this, I turn off the oven at the end of the baking time and leave the pastry to cool inside. The residual heat evaporates the remaining water and helps the buns stay crisp.

MY FAVOURITE CHOUX PASTRY

MAKES ENOUGH
DOUGH FOR
12 ÉCLAIRS
OR ABOUT 30
PROFITEROLES

75g butter, diced

1 tsp caster sugar

50g plain flour

50g strong bread flour

3 eggs

1. Preheat the oven to 180°C/160°C fan/gas 4. Line a large baking sheet with baking parchment.

2. Place the butter, sugar and 125ml of water into a small saucepan over a medium-high heat. Bring the mixture to a rolling boil and when all the butter has melted, add the flours and vigorously beat the mixture with a wooden spoon until a smooth ball of dough forms.

3. Keep the pan on the heat and stir rapidly for a further minute. This cooks the flour and helps dry out the dough so it absorbs more egg, which in turn helps the pastry to expand properly when baked. Tip the dough into a bowl and leave it to cool until it has stopped steaming. The dough needs to cool properly so that when you add the egg it doesn't scramble.

4. Beat the eggs together briefly in a small jug. Add the eggs to the cooled dough in three separate additions, beating well between each one with a wooden spoon or spatula. It can be quite difficult to work in, but keep mixing and it will turn into a thick paste. You might not need to add all of the egg – when you are adding the final amount you want to add just enough so the dough falls off the spoon and leaves a 'v' shape. The choux dough is now ready to use to create all kinds of masterpieces; try one of my recipes on the following pages for inspiration.

TURKISH DELIGHT PROFITEROLES

These profiteroles are drizzled in a sticky rose syrup and garnished with vibrant pistachio nuts, all coated in a light dusting of icing sugar. I like to include small pieces of real Turkish delight too, for a contrasting texture, but they are not essential.

People often say that they aren't sure about rose as a flavouring, but when I ask if they like Turkish delight (which is rose-flavoured), the answer is almost always yes. It doesn't have a soapy or overwhelming flavour; in fact, if used correctly it is delicate and floral.

MAKES ABOUT 30

1 x My Favourite Choux Pastry recipe (page 152)

FILLING
200ml double cream
1 tsp rosewater
2 tbsp icing sugar

TOPPING
100g caster sugar
1 tsp rosewater
75g pistachio nuts, chopped
Icing sugar and Turkish delight cubes, to serve (optional)

1. Preheat the oven to 200°C/180°C fan/gas 4 and line a large baking sheet with baking parchment.

2. Make the pastry and spoon the mixture into a large piping bag. Snip the tip off and pipe about 30 small balls of the pastry onto the baking sheet, leaving space for them to spread out, then bake for 20–25 minutes or until risen and a dark golden brown in colour. If they are too pale, they will become soft before they are filled with cream. Turn the oven off and leave the profiteroles in the oven to dry out and cool completely.

3. To make the filling, whip the cream with the rosewater and icing sugar until it forms soft peaks then spoon into a piping bag. Pierce the bottom of each cooled profiterole with a skewer, snip the tip off the piping bag and fill each one with the rose cream.

4. Make a rose syrup by putting the caster sugar and rosewater into a saucepan with 75ml of water and heating it gently. Stir until all the sugar has dissolved, then bring to the boil for around a minute so that the mixture thickens slightly. Remove from the heat and leave to cool.

5. When you are ready to serve the profiteroles, pile them on a large plate. Pour the rose syrup over the top, then sprinkle over the pistachios and Turkish delight cubes (if using). Dust with icing sugar just before serving.

IRISH CREAM ÉCLAIRS

Coffee éclairs are well loved all over the world, and my Irish cream filling is a twist on this classic. Baileys has a great creamy flavour, so it is no surprise that it works perfectly in lightly whipped cream. If you don't like cooking with alcohol, you can fill these éclairs with fresh cream instead.

MAKES 12

1 x My Favourite Choux
   Pastry recipe (page 152)

1 egg, beaten

FILLING

100g mascarpone

200ml double cream

75ml Baileys

TOPPING

1 tsp instant coffee granules
   dissolved in 2 tbsp of
   boiling water

200g fondant icing sugar or
   icing sugar

Cocoa powder, to dust

You will also need a piping
bag and an open star nozzle.

1. Preheat the oven to 180°C/160°C fan/gas 4 and line a large baking sheet with baking parchment.

2. Make the pastry and spoon it into a large piping bag fitted with an open star nozzle. Using the star nozzle helps the choux pastry expand in a more even way.

3. Line a ruler up next to the baking sheet and pipe 12 x 10cm éclairs onto the sheet, making sure to leave enough space between each one for them to expand during baking. Use a wet finger to smooth over any bumps. Glaze each éclair with the egg using a pastry brush.

4. Bake for 25–30 minutes until golden brown and well risen. Turn the oven off and leave the éclairs in the oven to dry out and cool completely.

5. Whip the mascarpone and cream together with the Baileys until it thickens, then spoon this mixture into a piping bag. Use a skewer to pierce the cooled éclairs at one end and fill with the Baileys cream.

6. To make the topping, add the coffee to the icing sugar a little bit at a time until you get a paste that is just thick enough to spread onto the eclairs without it dripping down the sides. Dip the éclairs top down into the icing or use a small palette knife to spread it over each one then dust with cocoa powder. These are best served as soon as possible, as the cream will make the pastry soft.

RHUBARB CRUMBLE CHOUX BUNS

The shortbread-like crumble topping on these choux buns not only tastes delicious, but helps the choux pastry to expand into perfect rounds. I fill them with a light crème pâtissière and sticky rhubarb compote so they are packed full of flavour.

MAKES 15

1 x My Favourite Choux
  Pastry recipe (page 152)
Icing sugar, to dust

CRUMBLE TOPPING
75g plain flour
75g caster sugar
75g butter, diced

CRÈME PÂTISSIÈRE
350ml whole milk
1 tsp vanilla bean paste
4 egg yolks
30g cornflour
75g caster sugar
200ml double cream

COMPOTE
200g rhubarb
75g caster sugar
100ml orange juice

You will also need an electric hand-held whisk.

1. Start by making the crumble topping. Put the flour and sugar in a bowl and mix until completely combined. Add the cubes of butter and rub into the dry ingredients until the mixture resembles large breadcrumbs. Press the mixture together into a ball using your hands and then roll it out into a thin sheet between two pieces of cling film or baking parchment. It should be around 2mm thick. Put into the freezer to harden.

2. Preheat the oven to 180°C/160°C fan/gas 4 and line two baking sheets with baking parchment.

3. Make the pastry and transfer to a piping bag. Snip off the tip of the bag and pipe 15 x 4cm circles onto the baking sheets. You could use a template like the one I use in my macaron recipe (see page 81) to make it easier.

4. Remove the crumble layer from the freezer and use a 4cm cutter to make 15 circles. Put one onto the top of each pastry round; it will look quite odd sitting on the top, but it will melt around the pastry in the oven. Put the sheets into the oven and bake for 20–25 minutes until risen and golden on top. Turn off the heat and leave the buns to cool completely in the oven.

5. In a small saucepan, heat the milk and vanilla bean paste together over a low heat until steaming and almost boiling.

6. Meanwhile, use an electric hand-held whisk to beat together the egg yolks, cornflour and caster sugar in a jug until a thick paste forms. Keep whisking until the mixture has turned slightly lighter in colour.

7. When the milk is steaming, pour a small amount into the egg mixture and quickly whisk it in. If you aren't quick enough, the hot milk will scramble the egg. Gradually add the rest of the hot milk, whisking all the time, until it is all incorporated.

8. Pour the crème pâtissière back into the saucepan and continue to heat, whisking all the time, until it becomes a very thick paste. This can happen very suddenly, because as soon as the eggs get to the right temperature

they set and thicken the mixture. Transfer the thickened mixture into a jug, then cover with cling film and chill for at least one hour or until cool.

9. To make the rhubarb compote, chop the rhubarb into small pieces and place into a saucepan with the sugar and orange juice. Simmer over a medium heat, stirring occasionally, until the rhubarb pieces have completely broken down and the mixture is thick and sticky. Spoon into a small jar or container and refrigerate until ready to use.

10. Whip the double cream into soft peaks. Stir the cool crème pâtissière briefly to loosen it, then gently fold in the whipped cream until the mixture is light and but still thick enough to pipe into the buns. Try not to over-fold here or you will risk making the filling too runny. Transfer to a piping bag.

11. Use a skewer to make a small hole in the bottom of the buns then snip the tip off the piping bag and fill each a third full with crème pâtissière, then pipe in a layer of rhubarb, followed by more crème pâtissière until the bun is completely full. Dust with icing sugar before serving.

SHORTCRUST PASTRY

This is the pastry used to make pies and tarts.

It is a curious concept, because a shortcrust pastry shell should be both strong enough to hold a filling well, but also crumbly enough to melt in the mouth when you eat it. You need to find the perfect balance between strength and texture.

To keep the pastry short, and stop it becoming tough and chewy, the gluten strands in the flour need to be 'shortened' to prevent them developing a strong network. Since gluten networks need water to form, you can stop them with fat: by rubbing the butter into the flour, each flour particle becomes coated in fat, the gluten proteins can't join together as well, the chains are shorter and this results in a much more crumbly texture. Make sure that the butter is completely rubbed into the flour and you add as little water as possible to create the best quality pastry. The addition of ground nuts or cocoa powder works wonders in breaking up the gluten structure too, so I would recommend including them as well.

Pastry does like to be kept cold and it is a common saying that if you have warm hands, you can't make good pastry. This isn't strictly true, although if you do have abnormally warm fingers I would suggest working quickly or using a food processor to stop the butter from melting. The chilling stages are also really important because the fat needs to solidify or it won't hold its shape properly when you come to bake it. Finally, resting the dough allows the gluten that has developed (you need a small amount to hold the dough together) to relax, which stops the pastry shrinking when you put it into the tart shell.

MY FAVOURITE SWEET SHORTCRUST PASTRY

**MAKES ENOUGH
TO LINE A 23cm
TART TIN**

200g plain flour
20g ground almonds
35g icing sugar
125g cold butter, diced
1 egg, separated

1. Put the flour, almonds and icing sugar into a large bowl and mix together until well combined.

2. Add the butter to the dry ingredients and rub into the flour until you get a mixture that looks like fine breadcrumbs.

3. Add the egg yolk (save the white for glazing) and 1 tablespoon of cold water and stir into the flour with a round-ended knife. The mixture will start to clump together after you have mixed for a minute or so, but there will still be some floury patches in the bowl. Turn the contents of the bowl onto a large piece of cling film and knead briefly until all the pastry has come together into a ball. Wrap in the cling film and place in the fridge for 30 minutes, or until you are ready to use it.

BLIND BAKING

To avoid the dreaded soggy pastry bottom, blind baking is a great technique to master. Baking the pastry case before any filling has been added allows it to crisp up, stopping any wet fillings seeping through.

1. Preheat the oven to 190°C/170°C fan/gas 5. Roll out the chilled pastry between two pieces of cling film until it is a few centimetres larger than your tin. You could also do this on a floured surface, but the pastry is so fragile I find it easier to handle between cling film. Peel off the top layer of cling film then invert the pastry circle into the prepared tart tin, gently pressing it into all the edges. Put the pastry-lined tin into the fridge for at least 30 minutes before baking.

2. Remove the cling film from the pastry, prick the base all over with a fork then line the inside with baking parchment and baking beans (you could also use uncooked lentils or rice if you don't have baking beans – anything that will weigh the paper down).

3. Bake for ten minutes, then carefully remove the paper and beans and bake for a further ten minutes, until the base is crisp. You are now ready to fill the case.

LEMON AND ELDERFLOWER TART

Elderflower has a delicate, floral flavour that works really well in this simple lemon tart. You need to be very careful when handling the pastry base, because any cracks will mean the filling will leak out in the oven. If you notice any gaps appearing after blind baking the tart, use leftover pastry dough to patch up the base.

SERVES 10

Butter, for greasing

1 x My Favourite Sweet Shortcrust Pastry recipe (page 161)

3 eggs

125g caster sugar

Zest and juice of 3 unwaxed lemons

150ml double cream

75ml elderflower cordial

Icing sugar, to dust

You will also need a 23cm loose-bottomed tart tin.

1. Butter a 23cm loose-bottomed tart tin, make the pastry, then use it to line the tin and blind bake it according to the instructions on page 161. Lower the oven temperature to 170°C/150°C fan/gas 3.

2. Lightly whisk together the eggs, sugar and lemon juice, then add the cream and elderflower cordial. Stir in two-thirds of the lemon zest, reserving the rest for the top. Try to pop any bubbles that appear on the surface with a skewer or skim them off with a spoon.

3. Pour half the lemon mixture into the tart case then put it in the oven. Once it is safely in, fill it completely to the top with the rest of the mixture (this half and half approach helps to prevent spillage) then bake for 30–35 minutes or until the tart has just set. It should still have a slight wobble in the middle.

4. Leave the tart to cool completely before removing it from the tin and chilling it in the fridge. To serve, dust with icing sugar and the remaining lemon zest and if you like you can add a big dollop of mascarpone mixed with whipped cream on the side.

MANGO AND LIME MERINGUE PIE

There is something about meringue pies that gets people excited. Breaking through the billowy cloud-like topping to get to the layer of fresh, fruity curd brings a smile to my face, and I can never resist a slice. I use Italian meringue for the topping because the hot sugar syrup cooks the egg white during the whisking process. It also has a slightly firmer texture than classic French meringue, which makes the pie easier to slice.

SERVES 10

1 x My Favourite Sweet
   Shortcrust Pastry recipe
   (page 161)

Butter, for greasing

FILLING

250g ripe mango, peeled,
   stone removed and cut
   into pieces

Zest and juice of 2 unwaxed
   limes

20g cornflour

150g caster sugar

3 medium egg yolks, beaten

50g unsalted butter, cubed

**ITALIAN MERINGUE
TOPPING**

225g caster sugar

3 egg whites

You will also need 23cm loose-bottomed tart tin, a stand mixer or electric hand-held whisk and a sugar thermometer.

1. Make the pastry and butter a 23cm loose-bottomed tart tin. Blind bake the case according to the instructions on page 161.

2. To make the filling, purée the mango, lime zest and juice by whizzing them in a blender for a few minutes until smooth. If you don't have a blender, you could use a hand-held blender or push the mixture through a sieve. Put the purée into a saucepan over a medium heat and whisk in the cornflour.

3. Whisk in the sugar and egg yolks, then add the butter. Continue to heat the mixture, whisking all the time, until the butter has melted. Cook for a further five minutes or until the curd has thickened significantly and the whisk leaves an obvious trail when you drag it through the mixture. Pour into the baked tart case and chill for at least an hour to set.

4. For the Italian meringue topping, put the sugar into a small saucepan with 175ml of water over a medium heat and stir until the grains of sugar have dissolved. Then bring the mixture to the boil.

5. Whilst the syrup is heating up, whisk the egg whites in a clean, grease-free bowl into soft peaks using an electric hand-held whisk or a stand mixer. When the sugar syrup reaches 118°C, pour it gradually down the side of the bowl into the whites, whisking all the time. Continue to whisk the meringue for ten minutes until it is really thick and glossy. Spoon onto the set filling, using the back of a spoon to swirl it right into the edges of the pie. Before serving, bake the pie at 200°C/180°C fan/gas 6 for 5–10 minutes, or use a blowtorch, just to lightly brown the top.

BLACKCURRANT AND CHOCOLATE MOUSSE TART

Chocolate mousse is a classic dessert, but I find it can often be too rich on its own. The sharpness of the blackcurrant layer cuts through the dark chocolate, making this tart really refreshing. Blackcurrants have quite a short season, so if you can't get them use blackberries instead, or even frozen forest fruits.

SERVES 10

1 x My Favourite Sweet
  Shortcrust Pastry recipe
  (page 161)

20g cocoa powder

Butter, for greasing

JAM LAYER

250g blackcurrants or
  blackberries, fresh or
  frozen

100g caster sugar

MOUSSE

200g dark chocolate,
  chopped

2 medium eggs, separated

4 tbsp caster sugar

250ml double cream

TO DECORATE

Fresh berries

Icing sugar

You will also need a 23cm loose-bottomed round or 36 x 12cm rectangular tart tin and an electric hand-held whisk.

1. Make the pastry, swapping the ground almonds for the same weight in cocoa powder, and butter a round (or rectangular) 23cm loose-bottomed tart tin. Line the tin with pastry and blind bake according to the instructions on page 161.

2. To make the jam, put the fruit, sugar and 100ml of water into a pan and boil for 10–15 minutes until the mixture is thick and glossy. If you put a small amount onto a cool plate and leave it for a few minutes, it should feel sticky rather than wet. Press the hot mixture through a sieve into a small jug, squeezing every bit of juice from the berries. You will be left with a thick pulp which you can discard and a jugful of smooth liquid.

3. Pour the blackcurrant liquid into the tart case and tilt the tin around so it coats the bottom completely. Put to one side while you make the mousse.

4. To make the mousse, melt the chocolate in the microwave or in a heatproof bowl over a pan of simmering water, then allow to cool slightly.

5. Using an electric hand-held whisk, beat the egg whites in a clean, grease-free bowl to soft peaks then add the sugar one tablespoon at a time, whisking throughout, until the mixture looks thick and glossy, a little like a meringue. Use the same whisk to beat together the egg yolks and cream in a large bowl, then fold in the melted chocolate.

6. Spoon the egg-white mixture onto the chocolate mixture and gently fold them together. You don't want to over-mix or the mousse will be too dense; just fold until all the white lumps of egg disappear.

7. Pour the mixture into the tart tin and use a spatula to smooth over the top. Allow to chill for at least two hours to set properly, but remove from the fridge 30 minutes before serving to get the best texture. Decorate with fresh berries and a dusting of icing sugar.

ROUGH PUFF PASTRY

If you buy your puff pastry instead of making it from scratch, you are in good company.

Making proper puff pastry takes time and effort, and involves bashing a lump of solid butter into a thin layer which is what puts a lot of people off having a go. My recipe is a rough puff pastry, so it takes half the time. Admittedly, it is still fairly time-consuming, so it's something I'd usually only make when I've got a little bit of extra time on my hands.

To get great layers in your pastry, you need to leave large chunks of butter. It seems unnatural, but the pockets of fat separate the dough, making the pastry flaky. As you roll and fold, thin layers of dough and thin layers of fat begin to build up. When baked, the layers of fat melt and the water in the dough evaporates creating steam. The steam then fills the gaps left by the melted fat, this pushes the layers apart and eventually the structure sets, creating the buttery, flaky texture.

Using strong flour helps keep the dough from tearing and creates more defined layers. Finally, keep in mind that the cooler your ingredients are, the better your pastry will be. If the fat melts too early, you will lose the layers you have built up, so make sure the dough is properly chilled at all times.

MY FAVOURITE ROUGH PUFF PASTRY

MAKES 500g

200g strong bread flour,
plus extra for dusting
200g cold butter, cubed
100ml ice-cold water

1. Sift the flour into a bowl and add the cubes of butter. Gently squash the butter between your fingers, loosely breaking it up and rubbing a little bit of it into the flour. You want to see large chunks of butter.

2. Using a round-ended knife, stir in the 100ml of ice-cold water, a tablespoon at a time, until a rough dough forms. You might not need all the water; you want a firm rather than wet dough.

3. Turn the mixture out onto a lightly floured surface and mould into a rectangle using your hands. Wrap the pastry in cling film and chill for 15 minutes.

4. Unwrap the chilled pastry and roll into a large rectangle on a floured surface. Fold the top third down and the bottom third up – as if you are folding a letter. Return to the fridge to chill for another 15 minutes.

5. Repeat the rolling and folding process three or four more times, turning the dough 90 degrees each time, until you can no longer see any large lumps of butter. Store in the fridge until you are ready to use it.

HOW TO FOLD PUFF PASTRY

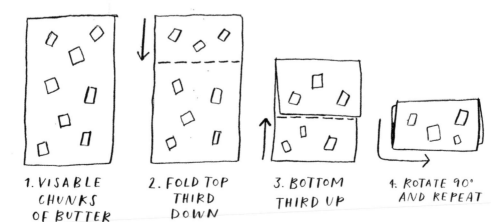

1. VISABLE CHUNKS OF BUTTER

2. FOLD TOP THIRD DOWN

3. BOTTOM THIRD UP

4. ROTATE 90° AND REPEAT

WHITE CHOCOLATE AND PEPPERMINT CREAM HORNS

Cream horns are a really fun thing to make with puff pastry. If you don't have cream horn moulds, you can fashion your own out of tin foil. Simply scrunch the foil into 12 conical shapes then wrap with another, smooth piece of foil to stop the pastry sticking too much. They should work just as well.

MAKES 12

1 x My Favourite Rough
   Puff Pastry recipe
   (page 169)
1 egg, beaten
50g caster sugar

TOPPING
100g white chocolate,
   chopped
75g chopped toasted
   hazelnuts

FILLING
75g white chocolate,
   chopped
300ml double cream
3 tbsp crème de menthe or
   ½ tsp peppermint extract

1. Make the pastry and line a large baking sheet with baking parchment.

2. Roll out the pastry into a large rectangle around 4mm thick. Use a sharp knife and a ruler to divide it into twelve 35cm x 2cm strips. Wrap each strip around a horn mould, starting at the tip and working upwards, with the pastry strip overlapping itself slightly at every turn. If you don't have 12 cream horn moulds or foil shapes, you can shape half, bake them, chill the moulds then shape the rest. Put the wrapped horns seam-side down on the baking sheet then chill for 10–15 minutes.

3. Preheat the oven to 200°C/180°C fan/gas 6. Brush the pastry horns with the beaten egg and sprinkle over the caster sugar. Bake for 15–20 minutes, or until the pastry is golden brown all over. You might need to rotate the baking sheet halfway through cooking to get an even bake. Allow the pastry to cool completely before removing it from the horn mould.

4. Melt the white chocolate for both the topping and the filling, either gently in the microwave or in a heatproof bowl over a pan of simmering water. Dip the end of each horn into the chocolate then roll it in the toasted hazelnuts. You should still have some white chocolate left after dipping all the horns. Leave the chocolate to harden on the horns whilst you make the filling.

5. Whisk together the cream, remaining white chocolate and mint flavouring of your choice until it forms soft peaks. Spoon into a piping bag, snip off the tip and fill each horn right to the top. These will keep in the fridge for up to three days but are best served immediately.

PEAR AND CASSIS TARTE TATIN

Tarte Tatin sounds fancy, but it is essentially a pastry version of an upside-down cake. It is baked with the pastry facing up, so there is no risk of a soggy bottom, and the pears gently caramelise underneath, creating a very tasty dessert.

SERVES 8

1 x My Favourite Rough
   Puff Pastry recipe
   (page 169)

4 large ripe pears

100g caster sugar

75g butter

2 star anise

1 cinnamon stick

3 tbsp crème de cassis

1. Make the pastry then chill it while preparing the rest of the ingredients.

2. Peel and core the pears, then cut them into quarters. You can prepare the pears in advance and keep them in the fridge; just squeeze over some lemon juice first to stop them from going brown.

3. Put the sugar, butter, star anise and cinnamon stick into a large ovenproof frying pan and place over a high heat until bubbling; this should take about five minutes. The frying pan will be going into the oven to bake later, so make sure it doesn't have a plastic handle or you'll be in trouble!

4. When the sugar has started to turn a golden colour, stir in the crème de cassis. The mixture will spit violently, so stir it in as carefully as you can. Cook for a further 3–4 minutes until the caramel is slightly thicker.

5. Remove from the heat, then arrange the pears with the long thin part pointing into the centre of the pan. At this point, you can refrigerate the frying pan until you are ready to bake or you can finish the tarte and bake it straight away.

6. Preheat the oven to 200°C/180°C fan/gas 6. Roll out the puff pastry into a large rectangle around 5mm thick. Cut a circle of pastry slightly larger than the frying pan – you want to be able to tuck it under the pears.

7. Lay the pastry circle over the pears and use your fingers to carefully tuck it underneath the pears at the edges. Work quickly if the caramel is still hot or the pastry will begin to melt. Bake for ten minutes, then turn the oven down to 170°C/150°C fan/gas 3 and bake for a further 20–25 minutes, or until the pastry is golden brown and crisp.

8. Allow the tarte to cool in the frying pan for a few minutes, then carefully turn out onto a large plate and serve straight away.

MARZIPAN PALMIER BISCUITS

Palmier biscuits are so simple to make, but look a lot more complicated than they actually are. Try my butterfly-shaped palmiers for a twist that children will love.

MAKES 24 BISCUITS OR 12 BUTTERFLIES

½ quantity My Favourite Rough Puff Pastry recipe (page 169)

250g marzipan

1 tsp ground cinnamon

50g caster sugar

1. Make the pastry then chill it.

2. Cover a work surface with baking parchment, put the chilled pastry on top then roll it out into a large rectangle about 5mm thick.

3. Roll the marzipan out into a rectangle about the same size as the pastry. I find this easiest to do between two pieces of cling film. Lay the marzipan sheet over the pastry and press it down firmly so the two stick together. Sprinkle over the cinnamon and caster sugar.

4. Starting with the long side of the rectangle, roll the pastry tightly into the centre of the baking parchment. Stop halfway, then repeat with the opposite side so you have a roll of pastry that looks like two scrolls stuck together. Wrap in the baking parchment and freeze for 20–30 minutes until the pastry is very firm.

5. While the pastry is chilling, line a baking sheet with baking parchment and preheat the oven to 180°C/160°C fan/gas 4.

6. Slice the palmier dough crossways into 1cm-thick pieces and arrange on the lined baking sheet. Bake for 10–15 minutes, or until the marzipan is golden brown and bubbling and the pastry is crisp. Leave them to cool completely before trying to remove from the baking parchment or they will get stuck.

TWIST: BUTTERFLY PALMIER BISCUITS

Make the recipe above up to step 3. Follow a similar process, but make one roll slightly larger than the other so when sliced, the bottom coil will be smaller than the top one. Chill and slice the dough as specified above but use a beaten egg to stick two of the palmiers together, flat side in the middle, so the circles become the 'wings'. Make some small antennae using offcuts of pastry and stick them to the top of each butterfly with more beaten egg, then bake as above.

DESSERTS

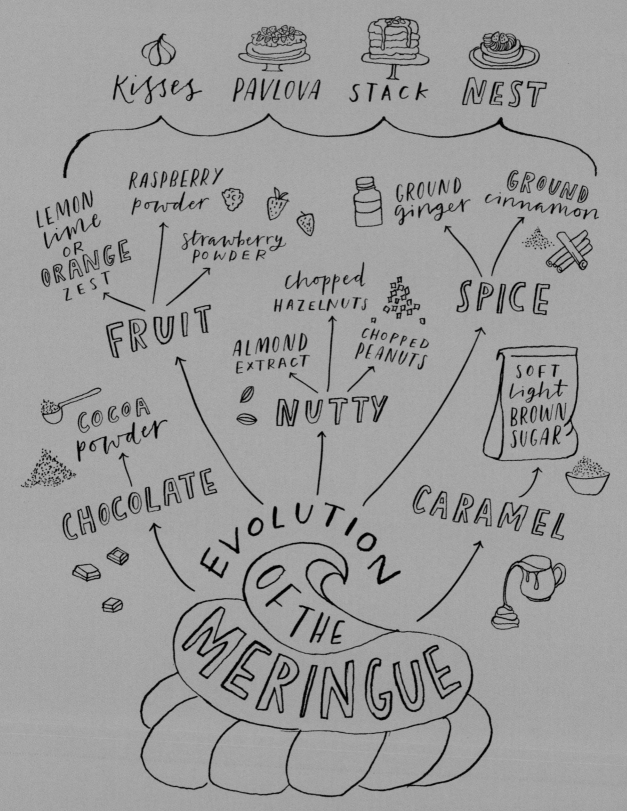

KISSES   PAVLOVA   STACK   NEST

LEMON lime OR ORANGE ZEST

RASPBERRY powder

strawberry POWDER

FRUIT

GROUND ginger   GROUND cinnamon

SPICE

chopped HAZELNUTS

ALMOND EXTRACT

CHOPPED PEANUTS

NUTTY

COCOA powder

CHOCOLATE

SOFT Light BROWN SUGAR

CARAMEL

EVOLUTION OF THE MERINGUE

MERINGUE

Meringue is incredibly versatile — think Eton mess, pavlova or lemon meringue pie.

It is also one of my favourite examples of the chemistry of cooking: you start with just two ingredients, and create something entirely different from the original materials. Let me explain how it works.

Egg white is a mixture of proteins and water molecules. When whisked, the proteins unfold and bubbly pockets of air are forced into the structure. The unfolded proteins bond together creating a 'scaffolding' that holds onto the air. You need to whisk the egg whites into stiff peaks that don't move when you tip the bowl upside down. If you don't whisk in enough air, you will have trouble maintaining volume when you add the sugar and the meringue might collapse.

Once the air has been locked in, the sugar is added and, as well as making the meringue taste delicious, it strengthens its structure. The sugar dissolves in the water in the egg whites and allows even more air to be incorporated. It is important that you whisk the meringue until all the sugar has dissolved or you are more likely to get cracks in your meringue as the sugar 'weeps' (leaks out) during the baking process. Heating the sugar first helps it to dissolve more quickly.

Finally, when you bake the meringue the heat causes the water to evaporate, the air pockets to expand and the protein structure to set. If you bake the meringue at too high a temperature, the outside of the meringue will set before all the water has evaporated, which will leave your meringue with a soggy middle. Baking the meringue for a long time at a low temperature will cook the meringue evenly, leaving you with a soft, chewy middle and a crisp shell — exactly how a meringue should be!

MY FAVOURITE MERINGUE

The ingredients for a meringue are very simple; you need double the weight of sugar to egg whites. It is easy to make any quantity of meringue if you follow this 2:1 ratio.

MAKES 1 LARGE PAVLOVA OR 12 SMALL NESTS

300g caster sugar
150g egg whites, (from about 5 eggs)

You will also need a stand mixer or an electric hand-held whisk.

1. Preheat the oven to 200°C/180°C fan/gas 6 and line a large baking sheet with baking parchment.

2. Pour the sugar onto the sheet and spread it out into an even layer. Warm in the oven for 5–6 minutes, until it feels hot to the touch and the very edges of the sugar are starting to melt.

3. While the sugar is heating up, put the egg whites into a large clean and grease-free bowl or the bowl of a stand mixer. You'll need an electric hand-held whisk or stand mixer to get the volume required for great meringue; don't try to do it by hand. Whisk the whites until they form stiff peaks. You should be able to tip the bowl upside down without anything falling out – when you can do this you know it is ready.

4. Carefully whisk the hot sugar into the egg whites, adding a spoonful at a time and fully mixing in each one before adding the next. If you do this too quickly, the meringue may collapse, so add it slowly and carefully. Avoid using any of the melted sugar from the edges of the baking sheet – this will not dissolve properly.

5. When all the sugar has been added, turn the mixer speed up and whisk for 8–10 minutes or until the mixture is really thick and glossy. If you rub a small amount between your fingers, you shouldn't be able to feel any grains of sugar but, if it still feels gritty, continue to whisk for a few more minutes until it feels smooth. Your meringue is now ready to bake – use it in one of the recipes on the following pages.

CREAM TEA MERINGUES

When you fancy something a little different from a scone, try these mini nests. Filled with thick clotted cream and topped with fresh berries, they are a perfect treat.

MAKES 12

1 x My Favourite Meringue
recipe (page 178)
12 tbsp clotted cream
Strawberries and
raspberries, to decorate

You will also need a stand mixer or an electric hand-held whisk.

1. Preheat the oven to 120°C/100°C fan/the lowest gas mark and line a large baking sheet with baking parchment or with a reusable baking sheet. Make the meringue, spoon into a piping bag and snip off the tip.

2. Pipe a 5cm circle of meringue mixture onto the parchment, then pipe two or three rings around the edge to create a nest. Repeat with the remaining mixture, then bake for 1½ hours or until they are crisp and peel off the paper without sticking. Leave to cool completely. If you aren't eating them straight away, the meringues will keep in an airtight container for up to two weeks.

3. When the meringue nests are cool and you are ready to eat/serve them, slice the strawberries into thin strips and halve the raspberries.

4. Spoon a tablespoon of clotted cream into each meringue, pile the berries on top and serve immediately.

SALTED CARAMEL AND APPLE PAVLOVA

This sticky, sweet pavlova is a reminder of everything that is great about autumn. Brown sugar meringue, which has delicate toffee notes, makes the perfect base for a pile of baked apples drenched in salted caramel sauce. You can put the apples onto the pavlova when they are still warm, but it will make the cream melt so it won't look quite as pretty.

SERVES 10

1 x My Favourite Meringue recipe (page 178)
200g soft light brown sugar

TOPPING
500g apples, cored and cut into wedges
25g butter, cut into small pieces
100g brown sugar
300ml double cream

CARAMEL
200g caster sugar
25g butter
50ml double cream
Pinch of sea salt

You will also need a stand mixer or electric hand-held whisk.

1. Preheat the oven to 120°C/100°C fan/the lowest gas mark and make the meringue, replacing 200g of the caster sugar with brown sugar. Pile into a large mound on a baking sheet lined with baking parchment and spread into a large circle.

2. Bake for three hours so the meringue is completely dried out and crisp all over. To ensure a crunchy shell and soft, chewy middle, I like to turn the oven off and leave the meringue to cool in the oven overnight. If you don't have time, just leave it to cool on the tray until completely cold.

3. To make the topping, turn the oven up to 200°C/180°C fan/gas mark 6. Put the apples into a roasting tray and sprinkle over the butter and sugar. Bake for 30 minutes, giving the apples a shake halfway through. When they are nicely caramelised, remove from the oven and set aside to cool.

4. Make the salted caramel by placing the caster sugar into a large, heavy-based saucepan. Add 4 tablespoons of water and stir until the sugar and water are well mixed.

5. Put the caramel mixture on the heat, bring to a low simmer and cook until it starts to change colour. Don't stir at this point or the sugar will crystallise and you will have to start again! You want the caramel to be a light amber colour (reading at around 165°C on a sugar thermometer if you have one).

6. As soon as the caramel turns a light amber colour, take the pan off the heat and stir in the butter. It will splutter and spit, so be careful when mixing. When the sauce is smooth, add the cream and salt and mix until combined.

7. Whip the remaining cream into soft peaks and spread over the top of the cooled meringue. Pile the apples on top of the cream, drizzle with caramel sauce then serve.

PEACH AND POMEGRANATE PAVLOVA

Pomegranate seeds look stunning sprinkled simply over the top of this pavlova. Their vibrant colour really lifts the dessert, and the way they burst in your mouth complements the chewy meringue beautifully. I use sliced tinned peaches when peaches are out of season; they work just as well.

SERVES 8

1 x My Favourite Meringue recipe (page 178)

2 tbsp freeze-dried raspberries, crushed to a fine powder

300ml double cream

4 ripe peaches, stoned and thinly sliced

1 pomegranate, deseeded

You will also need a stand mixer or electric hand-held whisk.

1. Preheat the oven to 120°C/100°C fan/the lowest gas mark and line a baking sheet with baking parchment or a reusable baking sheet.

2. Make the meringue mixture then sprinkle the raspberry powder over the top and fold through a few times. You want to see ripples of raspberry, so don't mix it in completely. Spoon onto the baking sheet and spread it out into a large rectangle that is the same thickness all over. Bake for three hours so the meringue is completely dried out and crisp. To ensure a crunchy shell and soft, chewy middle, I like to turn the oven off and leave the meringue to cool in the oven overnight. If you don't have time, just leave it to cool on the tray until completely cold.

3. Whip the cream into soft peaks and just before serving, spoon it onto the top of the meringue. Arrange the peach slices on top of the cream, fanning them out, then sprinkle over the pomegranate seeds.

MONT BLANC STACKED SHOWSTOPPER

The classic Mont Blanc combines meringue, sweet chestnut purée and lightly whipped cream. My version is slightly different: a towering stack of cocoa-swirled meringues are sandwiched together with a sweet chestnut cream and finished with dark chocolate curls, a perfect festive dessert.

SERVES 10

1 x My Favourite Meringue recipe (page 178)

2 tbsp cocoa powder, plus extra to dust

FILLING

1 x 212g tin sweetened chestnut purée

350ml double cream

1 tbsp icing sugar

100g dark chocolate shavings or 100g slab dark chocolate

You will also need a stand mixer or electric hand-held whisk.

1. Preheat the oven to 120°C/100°C fan/the lowest gas mark, cut four 20cm circles out of baking parchment and put them onto a baking tray.

2. Make the meringue mixture, sift the cocoa over the top and fold in as gently as possible – you don't want to knock out too much of the air you have just whisked in.

3. Divide the meringue mixture evenly between the four pieces of baking parchment and use a spatula to spread it right to the outsides of the circles. Dust the top with a little more cocoa powder and bake for 1½ hours until crisp. To ensure a crunchy shell and soft, chewy middle, I like to turn the oven off and leave the meringue to cool in the oven overnight. If you don't have time, just leave it to cool on the tray until completely cold.

4. To make the filling, whisk together the chestnut purée, double cream and icing sugar until the mixture forms soft peaks.

5. Place a meringue disc on a large plate and spread with quarter of the chestnut cream. Sprinkle a quarter of the chocolate shavings on top of the cream (if you can't buy shavings, you can make them by dragging a knife across the flat side of a bar of chocolate). Repeat with all four layers, then stack the discs on top of each other and serve immediately. You can store the dessert in the fridge for up to three days, but the longer you leave it the softer the meringue will become.

KEY LIME PIE CHEESECAKE

If you are looking for a really quick yet impressive dessert, this will become your new go-to. I use ginger biscuits to make the base – I love the punchy ginger flavour with the lime filling – but you could use plain digestives if you aren't a fan of ginger.

SERVES 8

BASE
200g ginger biscuits
75g butter, melted

FILLING
1 x 397g tin condensed milk
300g full-fat cream cheese
Zest and juice of 4 unwaxed
limes
200ml double cream

You will also need a 20cm pie dish or loose-bottomed tin.

1. Line the base of a 20cm pie dish or a loose-bottomed cake tin with a circle of baking parchment.

2. To make the base, blitz the ginger biscuits in a food processor until they resemble very fine crumbs. Pour the melted butter into the crumbs and blitz again until all the biscuit crumbs are coated in butter. Alternatively, put the biscuits into a plastic bag, use a rolling pin to crush them to a fine powder then put the crumbs into a bowl and stir in the butter. Press the mixture into the base and sides of the prepared tin, pressing firmly with the back of a teaspoon to make sure it sticks together, then chill for at least 30 minutes.

3. Whisk together the condensed milk and cream cheese until smooth. Stir in the lime juice and half the lime zest, then pour into the biscuit base. Ideally, refrigerate for at least two hours, but you could get away with serving this after 30 minutes if you are in a real rush!

4. Whip the double cream into soft peaks, and spoon or pipe it on top of the pie. Garnish with a sprinkle of the remaining lime zest before serving.

PEANUT BUTTER AND SOUR CHERRY CHEESECAKE

This is my ultimate cheesecake: sweet cream cheese, salty peanut butter and tart sour cherries all mingle together to create one perfectly balanced flavour sensation. It is set with gelatine, which means it takes a little longer to make, but the beautiful smooth texture makes it worth the wait.

SERVES 10

Butter, for greasing

CHERRIES
75g dried sour cherries, plus extra for decorating

1 tbsp caster sugar

1 tsp vanilla bean paste

1 tbsp kirsch (optional)

BASE
175g digestive biscuits

25g salted peanuts, plus extra for decorating

75g unsalted butter, melted

CHEESECAKE LAYER
400g full-fat cream cheese

150g caster sugar

2 egg yolks

250ml double cream

5 leaves gelatine

150g smooth peanut butter

CHOCOLATE TOPPING
75g dark chocolate, chopped

1 tbsp golden syrup

100ml double cream

You will also need a 20cm round springform tin.

1. Grease a 20cm springform tin and line with baking parchment.

2. Put the dried sour cherries into a small saucepan with the sugar, vanilla, and 1 tablespoon of water. If you are using kirsch, add this now. Bring to the boil and leave to simmer for 4–5 minutes. The cherries should soften and absorb some of the liquid. Set the pan to one side to cool.

3. To make the biscuit base, blitz the digestive biscuits and peanuts in a food processor until they resemble very fine crumbs. Pour the melted butter into the crumbs and blitz again until all the biscuit crumbs are coated in butter. Alternatively, finely chop the peanuts and place into a plastic bag with the biscuits, use a rolling pin to crush them to a fine powder, then put into a bowl and stir in the butter. Tip the crumbs into the base of the prepared tin, then press them down firmly with the back of a teaspoon to make sure they stick together, then chill for at least 30 minutes.

4. In a large bowl, whisk together the cream cheese, caster sugar and egg yolks until smooth. Stir in the cream until you get a thick but not stiff consistency.

5. Soak the gelatine leaves in cold water and allow to soften completely. This will take around five minutes. Melt the smooth peanut butter in the microwave in a medium bowl for about 30 seconds until it is even smoother. Squeeze the gelatine leaves to remove any excess water, then stir into the warm peanut butter until completely dissolved.

6. Spoon a few tablespoons of the cream cheese mixture into the peanut butter and mix well, before pouring all of the peanut butter mixture into the remaining cream cheese and stirring until completely smooth.

7. Drain the cherries then add half to the mixture and stir in. Spread onto the prepared biscuit base and use a spatula to smooth the top. Leave to set in the refrigerator, preferably overnight, but for at least four hours.

8. When the cheesecake feels firm enough to hold a layer of chocolate (usually after around two hours of chilling), make the chocolate topping. Place the chocolate, golden syrup and cream into a small bowl. Microwave on high for around one minute, removing from the microwave and stirring well every 15 seconds, until the mixture is smooth and no lumps of chocolate remain. Pour over the cheesecake, tilting the tin until the whole top is covered. Decorate with the remaining sour cherries and peanuts. Chill for two hours before serving.

ZEBRA CHEESECAKE

A really simple technique is used to create this spectacular cheesecake. It doesn't look much at first glance, but as soon as it is cut, all of its stripy secrets are revealed. I would really recommend using a hot knife to slice this, to make sure you get the clean, defined stripes – just put the blade of a metal knife in boiling water, dry it then clean it off between each slice. Repeat the heating process every few slices so the knife remains hot.

Cooking the cheesecake in a water bath seems like an odd idea, but it is an essential part of creating a smooth texture. It allows the cheesecake to cook slowly and evenly all the way around, so the edges do not brown or dry out too much.

SERVES 10

Butter, for greasing

BASE
200g digestive biscuits
75g butter, melted

TOPPING
500g full-fat cream cheese
100g soured cream or full-fat natural yoghurt
150g caster sugar
3 eggs plus 3 yolks
100g white chocolate, melted (page 113)
100g dark chocolate, melted

You will also need a 20cm round springform tin.

1. Preheat the oven to 170°C/150°C fan/gas 3. Grease the bottom of a 20cm springform tin and line with a circle of baking parchment.

2. To make the biscuit base, blitz the digestive biscuits in a food processor until they resemble very fine crumbs. Pour the melted butter into the crumbs and blitz again until all the biscuit crumbs are coated in butter. Alternatively, put the biscuits into a plastic bag and use a rolling pin to crush them to a fine powder then put the crumbs into a bowl and stir in the butter. Press the mixture into the base of the prepared tin, pressing firmly with the back of a teaspoon to make sure it sticks together, then chill for at least 30 minutes.

3. Beat the cream cheese, soured cream or yoghurt and caster sugar together until smooth, then carefully stir in the eggs and egg yolks. You don't want to beat in too much air or your cheesecake won't be smooth and creamy. Divide the mixture between two bowls then gradually stir the melted white chocolate into one bowl and the melted dark chocolate into the other. Don't pour the chocolates in all at once or you will cook the eggs.

4. Cover the bottom and outsides of the tin with one large sheet of tin foil, then repeat with a second piece. Covering it with foil serves two purposes: it stops the cheesecake leaking out and stops the water from getting in. Put the foil-wrapped tin into a roasting tray that is slightly larger than the tin.

5. Put a spoonful of the white chocolate mixture into the centre of the base then put a spoonful of dark chocolate mixture directly in the centre of the white chocolate. It should start spreading out, but if it doesn't, give

the tin a gentle shake. Continue to alternate spoonfuls of the mixtures inside each other until they are both used up. Give the tin a final shake to even out the top.

6. Put the roasting tin into the centre of the oven, then fill the roasting tin with boiling water. Stop pouring water in when it reaches halfway up the tin or it will be difficult to get out. Bake for 45–50 minutes. The outside of the cheesecake should be firm, but the centre should have a slight wobble. Take the roasting tin out of the oven and, using oven gloves, carefully lift out the cheesecake tin. Unwrap it, then put it on a cooling rack to cool down. When the cheesecake is cool, put it into the fridge. If you can, leave it overnight to firm up completely. Serve chilled.

PEACH AND ALMOND CRUMBLE

I make my crumbles a little differently, preferring to roast the fruit first until it caramelises to bring out the sweet flavours and dry it out slightly, allowing the juices to turn into sticky syrup. I also cook the crumble topping separately so you get crunch in every bite, avoiding any undercooked patches. Admittedly, it is more effort than throwing it all into one dish, but I think you'll agree that it is so worth it. You can make the component parts in advance then assemble them when you are ready to serve; the crumble topping can even be frozen.

SERVES 4-6

FILLING
6-8 large peaches, about
    1kg
50g caster sugar
50ml amaretto

TOPPING
175g butter
175g plain flour
150g soft light brown sugar
25g rolled oats
2 tbsp flaked almonds

1. Preheat the oven to 180°C/160°C fan/gas 4 and butter an ovenproof dish.

2. Cut the peaches into quarters and remove the stones. Arrange in the prepared dish, sprinkle over the sugar and pour in the amaretto. Bake in the oven for 30–35 minutes, or until the fruit is juicy and the edges are starting to caramelise. You can set the fruit to one side at this stage until you are ready to assemble the crumble.

3. To make the crumble topping, rub the butter into the flour until it starts to clump together and you can't see any large chunks of butter. Stir in the sugar, oats and almonds and mix with your hands. Spread the crumble out on a baking sheet and bake for 15 minutes or until just starting to go brown.

4. Ten minutes before you want to serve the crumble, turn the oven up to 200°C/180°C fan/gas 6. Sprinkle the crumble topping over the roasted fruit and bake for ten minutes to heat thoroughly. Serve bubbling hot with a generous amount of custard!

TWIST: RHUBARB AND STRAWBERRY CRUMBLE

Swap the peaches for 600g chopped rhubarb and 400g strawberries. Follow the same method as above, baking the rhubarb with 100g caster sugar for 25 minutes on its own before adding the strawberries for the final ten minutes. The fruit should look soft and slightly caramelised and a sticky syrup should have formed. Make the crumble topping, with or without the flaked almonds, and bake as above.

MELT-IN-THE-MIDDLE CHOCOLATE PUDDINGS

When I was 15, I made these puddings in a cookery competition, during which I was so engrossed in watching them bake that I left my oven gloves on an open hob and they caught fire. The entire school, judges and all, had to be evacuated. Much to my surprise and the other contestants' annoyance, I still managed to achieve second place and since then this dessert never fails to put a smile on my face. The combination of deep chocolate flavour and molten centre makes this the ultimate indulgent dessert. I serve mine with fresh berries to cut through the richness.

MAKES 8

125g butter, plus extra for greasing
Cocoa powder, to dust
200g dark chocolate, chopped
2 eggs plus 2 yolks
100g caster sugar
25g plain flour
Cream and berries, to serve

You will also need eight mini pudding or dariole moulds and an electric hand-held whisk.

1. Preheat the oven to 180°C/160°C fan/gas 4. Liberally butter eight mini pudding or dariole moulds and lightly dust the insides with cocoa powder. This makes the puddings easier to turn out once they are cooked. Cut a small circle of baking parchment the same size as the top of each mould and place inside each one to stop the puddings sticking.

2. Melt the butter and chopped dark chocolate in a large heatproof bowl set over a pan of simmering water. Stir together until there are no lumps of either remaining and the mixture is smooth.

3. Crack the eggs into another large bowl and add the extra yolks and the sugar. Use an electric hand-held whisk to whisk the mixture until it is thick, fluffy and very pale in colour. Fold in the melted chocolate using a spatula, then sift over the flour and mix well to combine. Don't worry if you knock out the air; you don't want the puddings to rise like a soufflé.

4. Spoon the mixture into the prepared moulds, filling each one two-thirds full. At this point, you could add a flavoured centre; see opposite for a few ideas.

5. Bake the puddings for 8–10 minutes. When they are ready, there should be a thin crust on the top but the centre should still have a slight wobble.

6. Leave the puddings to stand for two minutes before turning out. I run a small palette knife around the inside edge of each mould to loosen it slightly. If they do not turn out properly, or you want to play it safe, you can always serve the puddings in the mould and just dive straight in with a spoon. Serve with a nice dollop of cream and a few fresh berries.

TWISTS: FILLINGS

Try experimenting with different fillings! Push a few berries into the centre of each one before cooking, or try dropping in a teaspoonful of peanut butter or dulce de leche. A soft fondant mint or a Lindor chocolate ball also works really well.

SWEETS

S'MORES

MARSHMALLOW ICE-CREAM CONES

NOVELTY

LEMON AND Earl Grey

TEACAKES

chocolate AND RASPBERRY

Raspberry HEARTS

CUBES

SHAPES

COATING

CINNAMON STARS

SHERBET

POWDERED SUGAR

FREEZE-DRIED fruit

EVOLUTION of the MARSHMALLOW

WATER → LIQUID BASE ← TEA

fruit SMOOTHIE

FRUIT juice

SPICE-infused WATER

COFFEE

MARSHMALLOWS

Making homemade marshmallows is worth it just for the reaction you will get from friends and family when you tell them that you made them from scratch.

People can't believe that it is possible! Homemade marshmallows are a far cry from the ones you would normally buy – they are bouncier, denser and will melt in your mouth as you bite into them.

Once you've mastered the recipe on page 200, the days of bog-standard pink and white marshmallows are gone. You can flavour and coat the marshmallows with anything you like – the combinations are endless. Softening the gelatine can be done in any water-based liquid and will infuse the marshmallow with a delicate flavour, whether that be herbal tea or vibrant fruit juice. You can coat the marshmallows in all manner of different things, from fruit powders to spiced sugar. Remember to mix the coating you choose with a little cornflour to stop the marshmallows getting too sticky.

Making marshmallows can be quite a messy business, as the mixture has a habit of getting stuck in every little corner of the kitchen. Use any flavourless oil (sunflower or vegetable) to grease the spoons and spatulas as this will stop the kitchen becoming so sticky, and use boiling water to clean them when they get too covered. Make sure you oil the cling film that you use to line the tin too, or you won't be able to turn the marshmallow out properly.

A sugar thermometer is essential for making fail-safe marshmallows. If the syrup is not hot enough when you pour it in, the marshmallow will not set at all and, if it is too hot, it will set too firmly and won't have that lightness that you expect.

MY FAVOURITE MARSHMALLOWS

MAKES 24 SQUARES

125ml liquid flavouring of
   your choice, either at
   room temperature or
   slightly chilled (see pages
   198 and 201 for ideas)
2 x 12g sachets gelatine
   powder
450g caster sugar
150g golden syrup
cornflour or icing sugar,
   to dust

You will also need a sugar
thermometer and a stand
mixer or electric hand-held
whisk.

1. Pour the liquid into a large bowl or the bowl of a stand mixer and sprinkle over the gelatine. Set aside to allow the gelatine to soften and absorb all the liquid.

2. While the gelatine is soaking, put the caster sugar and golden syrup in a saucepan with enough water to cover (around 150ml). Cook over a low heat, stirring all the time, until the sugar has dissolved. As soon as there are no visible grains of sugar, turn up the heat and bring the mixture to the boil. Use a sugar thermometer to monitor it, and once it reaches 130°C take it off the heat and allow to cool for one minute so the mixture is no longer bubbling.

3. Whisk the gelatine/liquid mixture in a mixer, or with an electric hand-held whisk, on a medium speed. Add the sugar syrup, slowly pouring it down the side of the mixer bowl, whisking all the time. Try to avoid pouring directly onto the whisk or you will get grainy lumps of sugar in the marshmallow. The mixture should become pale and grow in volume like a very stiff meringue.

4. Once all the syrup has been added, continue to whisk for 5–10 minutes, until the mixture becomes really thick and cools a bit more. The mixture is ready when the outside of the bowl is just slightly warm and the marshmallow is starting to get really sticky. Use it in one of my recipes on the following pages or, to make simple cubes, use an oiled spatula to scrape it out of the bowl and spread the mixture into a square baking tray lined with oiled cling film. Leave to set for 1–2 hours at room temperature until the marshmallow feels firm. Dust in cornflour or icing sugar once set and cut into small cubes.

5. The marshmallows will keep for up to one week, and make great gifts.

MARSHMALLOW ICE-CREAM CONES

When my sister and I were young, my parents would bribe us into family shopping trips with the promise of being able to choose something from a local bakery at the end. We would always be immediately drawn to the most sugary of the lot: brightly coloured, sprinkle-topped ice-cream cones filled with marshmallow. You can use traditional or flat-bottomed cones and it is best to stand them in a container whilst the marshmallow sets or it will spill out.

MAKES 10

1 x My Favourite
  Marshmallows recipe
  (opposite)
10 ice-cream cones
Sprinkles and 10 Flakes,
  to decorate

1. Make the marshmallows, using whatever liquid you like for the base. See below for flavour ideas.

2. Use an oiled spatula to spoon the marshmallow mixture into a large piping bag, snip off the tip and fill the ice-cream cones all the way to the top, creating a slight dome.

3. Pour the sprinkles onto a plate and press the top of the marshmallow into them, rolling it around gently until the whole top is covered. Stick a Flake into each one and leave to set for 1–2 hours before enjoying as a great alternative to ice-cream.

TWIST: CLASSIC VANILLA

Mix 1 teaspoon of vanilla bean paste into 125ml of water and use it as the liquid base for the marshmallow filling. Top with multi-coloured sprinkles.

TWIST: LEMON SORBET

Use 125ml of cloudy lemonade as the liquid base for the marshmallow and top with white sprinkles and small pieces of candied lemon peel.

TWIST: STRAWBERRY AND BANANA

Use 125ml of strawberry and banana smoothie as the liquid base for the marshmallow and top each with pink sprinkles and a dried banana chip.

LEMON AND EARL GREY TEACAKES

Teacakes don't usually have tea in them, but I really love the subtle flavour of Earl Grey in both the marshmallow and the biscuit. Adding lemon to the biscuit brings out the spicy, citrus notes in the tea and also works really well with the dark chocolate. It is an unusual yet delicious combination.

MAKES 30

BISCUITS
200g butter, at room temperature
100g caster sugar
Zest of 1 unwaxed lemon
1 tsp vanilla bean paste
2 Earl Grey teabags
300g plain flour

TOPPING
1 x My Favourite Marshmallows recipe (see page 200)
125ml strong Earl Grey tea, cooled
200g dark chocolate, chopped
Lemon zest, to decorate

1. Line a large baking tray with baking parchment.

2. In a large mixing bowl, use an electric hand-held whisk or wooden spoon to cream the butter and sugar together until it is smooth and pale in colour. Stir in the lemon zest and vanilla paste then cut open the tea bags and sprinkle the contents into the mixture as well.

3. Mix in the flour very gently, taking care not to over-work the mixture as this will make the biscuits very chewy. Using your hands, take the dough and knead it gently into a ball with your palms. When it forms a smooth ball, wrap in cling film and chill in the fridge until you are ready to use it.

4. Preheat the oven to 180°C/160°C fan/gas 4. Roll the dough out to a 5mm thickness and use a 5cm round cutter to cut out 30 discs. Arrange on the lined baking tray and bake for 10–15 minutes or until the edges are just starting to turn brown. Allow to cool on the baking tray for a few minutes before transferring to a cooling rack.

5. Make the marshmallows using cool Earl Grey tea as the liquid then use an oiled spatula to spoon it into a large piping bag. Snip the tip off the bag and pipe tall peaks of marshmallow onto the top of each biscuit and leave to set for one hour before the next step.

6. Melt the dark chocolate (you could temper it if you want a more professional finish – see page 208) in the microwave or in a heatproof bowl over a pan of simmering water. Dip the teacakes in the melted chocolate, marshmallow side down. Sprinkle over the lemon zest and allow the chocolate to set before enjoying. These are perfect served with a cup of tea.

ROSE AND RASPBERRY MARSHMALLOW HEARTS

These delicately flavoured hearts are the best topping for a rich hot chocolate. Homemade marshmallows melt much more quickly and cover the top of the drink in a thick layer of gooey marshmallow, so you get a little taste in every sip.

MAKES 24

150g raspberries
½ tsp rosewater
1 x My Favourite
   Marshmallows recipe
   (page 200)
Pink gel food colouring
   (optional)
50g icing sugar
1 tbsp cornflour

You will also need a
23 x 35cm tin.

1. Put the raspberries in a saucepan with 50ml of water over a medium heat for five minutes, gently mashing the berries so they release their juice. Push the mixture through a sieve into a measuring jug then stir in the rosewater. If it doesn't reach 125ml, add enough water to make it up to this measurement.

2. Make the marshmallows, soaking the gelatine in 125ml of the raspberry and rose juice. Add a small amount of gel food colouring, if using, after the syrup in step 4.

3. Line a 23 x 35cm tin with oiled cling film. Use an oiled spatula to spread the marshmallow mixture into the tin then leave to set for 1–2 hours or until it feels firm.

4. Mix together the icing sugar and cornflour to make a powder. Turn the marshmallow out of the tin, peel off the cling film, then put the powder in a sieve and dust the whole slab of marshmallow with it.

5. Dip a small heart-shaped cutter in any flavourless oil and punch out heart-shaped marshmallows from the mixture. Dust in even more powder before serving – these are great in hot chocolate. They will keep for up to two weeks in an airtight container.

SCIENCE OF CHOCOLATE

The reasons why we all love chocolate so much don't need explaining — we are a culture that obsesses over the stuff.

There is so much information out there describing in detail exactly how to handle chocolate properly, but here I've summarised the basics of melting, tempering and making ganache into just a few easy stages.

MELTING

There are two common ways to melt chocolate: either in a bain-marie (a bowl set over a pan of simmering water) or in the microwave. People often worry about using the microwave to melt chocolate, believing that it can damage the chocolate; it won't damage it, but it will burn more easily, so make sure you stir the chocolate every 30 seconds. I always use the microwave to melt chocolate, especially for tempering, because chocolate and water don't mix. Using a bain-marie is more risky, because the smallest splash of water in the chocolate will cause it to seize (turn grainy and clump together). If this happens to your chocolate, it can no longer be used for coating. However, it does have other uses so don't throw it away! By whisking more water into the seized chocolate, you can bring it back to a smooth and shiny ganache that can be used in fillings or as a decoration.

TEMPERING

Tempering sounds scary, but it is just the process of heating and cooling chocolate to specific temperatures. Bars of chocolate that you buy are already 'in temper', meaning they are shiny and have a crisp snap. When you melt chocolate and allow it to cool without tempering it, the cocoa butter will solidify in an uncontrolled fashion, leading to the formation of the wrong type of fat crystals. This results in a dull appearance and the texture of the chocolate will be crumbly rather than smooth. A fat bloom (white streaks) might appear on the surface, which makes the chocolate a lot less appealing. If you ever have a bar of chocolate in your pocket on a hot day that melts, then pop it into the fridge to harden, you'll notice these changes. When you temper chocolate, you control the way the cocoa butter crystals solidify so you get the best-looking product when you work with it. There are several ways of tempering, but the 'seeding' technique is the one I like best.

You will need a sugar thermometer.

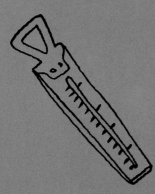

1. Chop the dark chocolate you need for the recipe into small, evenly sized pieces. Remove a third of the chocolate and put it into a separate bowl – you will add this back in later to bring down the temperature of the melted chocolate.

2. Melt the remaining chocolate until it reaches 45°C on a sugar thermometer. Stir in the chocolate you set aside earlier, until it has melted into the mixture. Adding unmelted, already tempered chocolate into melted chocolate encourages the proper fat structure to form.

3. When there are no lumps remaining in the chocolate, check the temperature. Dark chocolate should register 32°C on the thermometer. It is now ready to use, to coat truffles, make chocolate shapes or simply pipe onto the top of cakes.

GANACHE

Ganache is a simple mixture of cream and chocolate that sets firmly when allowed to cool. It is indulgent and so versatile – it can be used to fill cupcakes, make shiny glazes or even make soft truffles. I use a 1:1 ratio of cream to chocolate for a basic ganache. You can add butter for a softer set, or even a tablespoon of golden syrup to get a glossy shine.

MAKES ENOUGH TO COVER A 20cm CAKE

300g dark chocolate
300ml double cream

DARK CHOCOLATE

1. Chop the chocolate finely and put into a medium-sized bowl.
2. Heat the cream in a small saucepan until it just begins to simmer. When the cream is boiling, pour it over the chocolate chunks. The hot cream will melt the chocolate, so stir the two ingredients together until the chocolate has completely melted.
3. At this point, you have several options: pour the hot ganache straight onto cupcakes or larger cakes to get a shiny flat top; whip the ganache using an electric hand-held whisk to get a light, thick topping for a cake; or chill the mixture for a few hours in the fridge and use to make truffles (see my Amaretto Truffle recipe on page 212)
4. Ganaches can go wrong, sometimes for no apparent reason. If your ganache does split, add a tablespoon or two of warm water or milk. Whisk in the liquid and the ganache should return to its smooth and shiny self.

BUTTERSCOTCH ALMOND BAR

This chocolate bar is so simple to make, yet so delicious! The buttery caramel is made by boiling sugar, golden syrup and butter together, so it is much less likely to crystallise than regular caramel. This makes the recipe almost foolproof; just keep a close eye on it to make sure it doesn't burn and use a saucepan large enough for the mixture to bubble in.

MAKES 24

100g butter
275g caster sugar
50g golden syrup
75g flaked almonds, finely
   chopped
Pinch of sea salt
200g dark chocolate

You will also need a
20 x 35cm tin.

1. Line a 20 x 35cm tin with baking parchment.

2. Mix the butter, sugar and golden syrup in a large heavy-based saucepan and stir in 50ml of water. Bring to the boil and allow the mixture to bubble until it turns dark golden brown (150°C on a sugar thermometer, if you have one). It takes about ten minutes to reach this point on a fairly high heat.

3. Take the saucepan off the heat and add the almonds and sea salt. Stir well, then pour the hot mixture into the prepared tin. When the mixture has been cooling for around five minutes, it will begin to harden. At this point, use a sharp knife to divide the mixture into 24 squares. You don't need to cut all the way through – just marking it will make it easier to break into neat pieces when it is completely cool.

4. Temper the chocolate as described on page 208. Once tempered, dip each square into the chocolate and if you like you can make a pattern by dragging a fork across the top of the chocolate, then leave to harden completely on a piece of baking parchment. These will keep well in an airtight container for up to three weeks.

AMARETTO TRUFFLES

Crunchy pieces of amaretti biscuit gives these truffles a more interesting texture, and the bittersweet almond flavour of the amaretto makes them really indulgent. You can use any liqueur you like, or leave it out completely for a non-alcoholic version.

MAKES ABOUT 20

200g dark chocolate, finely chopped

200ml double cream

25g butter

2 tbsp amaretto

75g amaretti biscuits, crushed

Cocoa powder, to dust

1. Place the chocolate into a heatproof medium bowl.

2. Heat the cream and butter together in a small saucepan until it begins to simmer and the butter has completely melted. Mix in the amaretto and pour the hot mixture over the chocolate from step 1. Stir the ingredients together until the chocolate is completely melted and smooth, then mix in the crushed biscuits. Put the ganache in the fridge for at least two hours to firm up.

3. When the ganache is solid, shape it into about 20 small balls either using a melon baller dipped in boiling water or by piping small rounds. They don't need to be perfectly round as you will roll them in cocoa powder later. Return to the fridge for at least another hour.

4. Roll the chilled truffles in cocoa powder until they are round and completely covered, then chill until ready to eat. If they are a gift, package into small boxes or bags and keep in the fridge for up to a week until you are ready to give them.

PEANUT BUTTER BALLS

These peanut butter-filled chocolates are completely addictive. The slightly salty centre can be coated in chocolate and rolled in crushed peanuts, or left plain if you'd prefer. They make great gifts, and are a lot easier to make than classic truffles. If you are making them to give away, I'd strongly encourage making a double batch because they are so moreish that you won't have any left if you just make one!

MAKES 20

25g butter, softened
100g smooth peanut butter
25g soft light brown sugar
100g icing sugar
150g dark chocolate
50g salted peanuts

1. In a large bowl, beat together the butter and peanut butter until they are well combined. Stir in both the sugars until they are thoroughly incorporated and the mixture begins to clump together. It will be quite crumbly.

2. Roll the mixture between your hands into small evenly sized balls. Put onto a lined baking sheet and refrigerate for at least 30 minutes so they solidify completely before covering.

3. Whilst the peanut butter balls are chilling, temper the chocolate as described on page 208. Blitz the peanuts in a food processor until they are finely ground (alternatively, chop them finely using a sharp knife).

4. Spread the tempered chocolate on both palms of your hands then roll the chilled balls in your palms until they are completely covered with chocolate. Finally, roll them in the ground peanuts then put them onto a sheet of baking parchment to set completely before packaging up and giving as gifts (they will keep for up to a week in the fridge), or enjoying with a cup of coffee.

WHISKY AND GINGER TABLET

Family holidays in Cornwall would always begin and end with a trip to a fudge shop on Padstow harbour. My sister and I would browse the huge array of different fudges, ranging from classic to exotic, unable to choose. My dad would eventually decide for us, buying a bagful of sugary Scottish tablet. Deceptively ordinary-sounding, this harder version of fudge is buttery and crumbly. It is made in a similar way to fudge, but you stir the mixture while it is still hot so the sugar crystallises more quickly, creating a hard and crumbly tablet rather than a soft and smooth fudge.

MAKES 50 SQUARES

450g caster sugar
100ml whole milk
60g butter
200ml sweetened
    condensed milk
3 tbsp whisky
2 balls of stem ginger, from
    a jar in syrup, finely
    chopped

You will also need a 20cm square tin.

1. Line a 20cm square tin with baking parchment.

2. Put the caster sugar and milk together in a large saucepan and heat gently, stirring until all the sugar has dissolved. When the mixture looks smooth, stir in the butter and condensed milk and return to the heat.

3. Bring the mixture to the boil and allow it to bubble away for 15–20 minutes or until it turns a dark golden colour. If you have a sugar thermometer, you are looking for 118°C (the soft-ball stage). Stir the mixture occasionally to stop it from sticking to the bottom of the saucepan.

4. When the mixture is ready, stir in the whisky and ginger. Beat vigorously using a wooden spoon or electric hand-held whisk until it thickens and starts to harden on the edges of the pan. Spread into the prepared tin and leave to set. After 20 minutes, score the tablet into 50 squares so it is easier to break up later. The tablet will keep for up to one month in an airtight container.

ORANGE BLOSSOM AND DATE FUDGE

Creamy, smooth fudge isn't hard to make but it does require some patience. You need to ensure that the mixture comes up to temperature, or the fudge won't set properly. Another really important thing is to allow the mixture to cool after you have boiled it. If you start beating it too early, you will agitate the sugar crystals and your fudge will be gritty rather than smooth.

MAKES ABOUT 50 SQUARES

300ml double cream
350g caster sugar
1 tbsp golden syrup
50g butter
2 tsp orange blossom water
75g Medjool dates, destoned and chopped

You will also need a 20cm square tin and a sugar thermometer.

1. Line a 20cm square tin with baking parchment.
2. In a large saucepan, stir together the double cream, caster sugar, golden syrup and butter. Melt these ingredients over a medium heat, stirring until all the sugar has dissolved. Turn the heat up slightly and stick a sugar thermometer into the pan. Allow the mixture to boil until it registers 118°C on a sugar thermometer (this is called the soft-ball stage). Make sure you stir the mixture occasionally during the boiling process to stop the fudge catching on the bottom.
3. As soon as it reaches the desired temperature, take the pan off the heat and stir in the orange blossom water. Leave the pan to sit, undisturbed, until it cools to 50°C. This will take around 20 minutes. Don't be tempted to start stirring early, or the fudge will crystallise and be gritty.
4. When the mixture has cooled, add the chopped dates and beat the fudge vigorously until it begins to firm up and look glossy. When it has thickened, spoon the fudge into the prepared tin and leave to set at room temperature for at least three hours. When the fudge is firm, cut into pieces using a sharp knife. The fudge will keep for up to one month in an airtight container.

TWIST: CHOCOLATE AND HAZELNUT FUDGE

Try stirring 2 tablespoons of cocoa powder into the fudge at step 3 instead of the orange blossom water and stirring 75g toasted hazelnuts into the mixture at step 4 instead of the dates for a delicious nutty snack.

INDEX

ACKNOWLEDGEMENTS

If someone had said to me two years ago that I would have a published recipe book before I was 20, I would have thought they were completely out of their mind. I couldn't have dreamed of being in the position I am now, and I have so many people to thank for believing in me and supporting me this far.

Mum and Dad, thank you for being the most patient, unflappable parents in the world. Writing a book has been the hardest thing I have ever done, but without your constant encouragement, support and washing-up, these pages would be empty. Thank you for being my rock in late-night deadline panics and for sharing my joy in every successful bake – I hope you look back on this with fond memories.

Hannah, the kindest sister and best friend all rolled into one. Thank you for keeping me grounded and making me smile when I'm at my most stressed.

Grandparents, for always believing in me and being my PR team in Devon.

Michael, for being my constant calm and voice of reason. I could not have done this and kept my sanity without you.

Andy and Will, for being live-in recipe testers and surrogate brothers. You are the most rewarding people to bake for.

Louise, Alex, Sam and Lucy. Thank you for standing by me and maintaining friendship even when I didn't leave my kitchen for two months. You're all amazing.

Love Productions, for taking the risk that a 17-year-old could be let into the tent and not crumble under the pressure. I can never thank you enough. My fellow 2014 bakers: Nancy, Richard, Luis, Chetna, Kate, Norman, Diana, Iain, Jordan, Enwezor and Claire.

Thank you for being like a family and for being so much fun to share my time in the tent with.

Ascot Life Church, for the love, prayers and consumption of the majority of the food baked for this book.

Dr Green, Mr Chilton and my chemistry class, for putting up with my unreliable attendance and being my top market research group. Also thanks to Mrs Downy, Mrs McKinnon, Ms Witting, Mr Stagg, Mr Linton and all at Charters School for getting me here.

Emma Hurrell and friends at Tearfund, for taking me to Cambodia and showing me that the joy in baking can go so much further than these pages. Thank you for letting me serve as part of your campaign.

Dr David Grey and Professor Sandra Hill at Nottingham University, for giving up the time to check the scientific accuracy of my writing.

Claudia Young at Greene and Heaton, for motivating me to get my ideas down on paper. Thank you for helping me navigate through the world of media.

Tara Fisher and Annie Rigg, my fabulous photographer and food stylist duo. Thank you for bringing my food to life in absolutely beautiful ways and for making the shoots so much fun. Thanks also to Sue, Laura, Lola, Kathryn and Fran, and to Liz Belton for the gorgeous props.

Grace Cheetham, Georgina Atsiaris, James Empringham, Emily Barrett, Hannah Gamon and all at HarperCollins. Thank you for your constant patience and passion to turn my ideas into reality. I had no idea how much hard work and how many hours go into producing a book, and I couldn't have written it for a more supportive publisher. Thank you is not enough.